Yesterday's Heroes

Jane Hamilton

YESTERDAY'S HEROES

REVISITING THE OLD-TIME BASEBALL STARS

Marty Appel

WILLIAM MORROW AND COMPANY, INC.
New York

Library of Congress Cataloging-in-Publication Data

Appel, Martin.
    Yesterday's heroes / Marty Appel.
      p.   cm.
    ISBN 0-688-07516-9
    1. Baseball players—United States—Biography. I. Title.
    GV865.A1A67 1988
    796.357′092′2—dc19   88-3516
    [B]   CIP

Printed in the United States of America

First Edition

1 2 3 4 5 6 7 8 9 10

BOOK DESIGN BY RICHARD ORIOLO

FOR DEBORAH

ACKNOWLEDGMENTS

Special thanks to Bruce Danzls,
Mari Santana, Bill Guilfoile, and
Chuck Stevens.

CONTENTS

INTRODUCTION

*T*here are countless ways to measure baseball's charm, but one of my favorites is in a series of telephone messages I have received over the years from a close friend.

He never leaves his real name. It's always "Elio Chacon called," or "Mudcat Grant called," or "John Buzhardt called." Over the years I've had messages from Ruben Gomez, Jim Pisoni, Gail Harris, and Marcelino Lopez, not to mention Augie Donatelli, Dick Drott, and Choo Choo Coleman. How musical the names sound. And how come Jim Palmer never calls?

Such is the fantasyland of baseball, where names do not merely slip by, they become part of the game's history. To play in one single game means to be etched forever into *The Baseball Encyclopedia*. It probably means having a baseball card. And it probably means that someday your name might be left on a pink telephone message slip for me, evoking a smile and a memory of a wonderful game.

Oddly, few players get the same feeling as fans do from all this nonsense. Few players enter the game with much sense of history, and few leave it knowing they will be forever remembered. They are aware of baseball cards, but not all of them know of the collector's value and card shows that have become phenomena of the 1980s. And if they did, it might not matter much to them.

One wonders just how long this fascination with old baseball names has gone on. Did people leave funny phone messages, or sit around the old "hot stove league" in the 1920s and share remembrances of players from the 1890s?

Jim Turner, the oldest player interviewed for this book, has some thoughts on that. His playing career began in 1925.

"I know what you're talking about," he said, "because we did that, too. I'm talking about the players. In those days, there was so much more time for conversation. You'd travel by train, sit around, and talk. And if you were a baseball player, you'd talk baseball. But we'd mostly talk about the stars, not the journeymen. We had no image of them at all, so what could you discuss? You'd just pass on some of the crazy tales about characters like Rube Waddell and Germany Schaefer, but otherwise, if a player was not remembered for something odd, he'd leave no impression."

One suspects that fans had the same burden. Certainly, all of this collecting of cards and other souvenirs has really taken off in the 1980s and has made the more obscure players better appreciated.

The word among card collectors is "common." Some of the big stars from the 1953 Topps collection, for example, may be worth twenty-five or thirty dollars each. But "commons," just your ordinary nonstar player, are worth about a buck and a half.

This is a book about "commons," with a few exceptions. The big stars, who go on to become professional celebrities after their playing days, are not quite as interesting. We seem to hear of them all the time, whether from the broadcast booth, television commercials, celebrity golf tournaments, Old Timers' Days, or Hall of Fame inductions.

Many of the men in this book don't even come to mind when teams plan old timers' events. They have drifted from the glory of a baseball card to the life of just an "average" man. A common.

We gave some thought early on to including players from all sports in this collection. But somehow, the lasting remembrance isn't there in anything but baseball. There are no "cold stove" leagues for football fans to sit around and recall those great Chicago Cardinal offensive linemen of yesteryear.

For this collection of baseball figures we sought to build a cross section, representing different eras, different leagues, different levels of ability, different backgrounds, different positions. While we didn't necessarily always know how successful the players became, we wanted to come up with a fairly good cross section of success and disappointment, too. Nothing too dreadful, but what we thought might at least be representative of the fortunes and fates of the masses.

The players are only now catching up with their celebrity

among a new generation. It remains amazing to see what a tremendous impact baseball cards have had over the past forty years. Not only do they remain in circulation and thus keep the players on people's minds, but also they represent something for these players to hang their hat on as well. Very few claimed to be aware of *The Baseball Encyclopedia*. When asked how they'd go about finding out their lifetime statistics, most said they'd look on the back of a baseball card that was sent to them for an autograph. They didn't even seem to realize that few cards contain a player's lifetime final stats, for usually there is no card issued after he's retired or been released.

Few players, at the time they were released, believed it was over. Most thought they could have played another couple of years. But the passing of time makes them a bit wiser, and they have come to recognize that the game does indeed work as well as it does because new players replace old ones at just the right time.

Most of the players we caught up with were friendly and charming and delighted to spare the time to chat. Most indicated it was not a common occurrence, although getting mail from fans was common and made them feel important, and perhaps young again. A few players were less anxious to talk, and we even had a couple who claimed they were "tired of doing these things," although it was hard to believe that Rip Repulski really has to fight off interviewers.

These interviews were conducted during the 1987 season, so the ages, occupations, and states of health all reflect that time. The Giants, Twins, Cardinals, and Tigers were all heading for division championships in '87, and many of the players expressed strong rooting interests for the three veteran managers involved—Roger Craig of the Giants, Sparky Anderson of the Tigers, and Whitey Herzog of the

Cardinals. (Few knew the Twins' Tom Kelly.) It seemed that everyone roomed with Herzog or played with him at some point. He may well be the common link between Honus Wagner and Ozzie Smith.

Just one thing still bothers me: What if that really was Choo Choo Coleman who called me that day?

—MARTY APPEL

Larchmont, New York
January 1988

Cleveland Indians

TED ABERNATHY

BORN 1933
MINOR LEAGUES 1952–53,
   1956, 1958–63
SENATORS 1955–57, 1960
INDIANS 1963–64
CUBS 1965–66
BRAVES 1966
REDS 1967–60
CUBS 1969–70
CARDINALS 1970
ROYALS 1970–72

*D*espite a host of notable accomplishments as one of baseball's premier relief pitchers in an era when the talent first became appreciated, Ted Abernathy toiled away with that strange underhand delivery without cvcr hurling for a pennant winner and without ever pitching in the so-called glamor cities of the major leagues.

It is then not so surprising that in short order he faded from the memories of all but the most avid fans. The fact that he was twice the National League's "Fireman of the Year" hardly seems to matter.

What still gnaws at Ted—and who could blame him?—is the way it all ended. After all, how many pitchers conclude their careers with a 1.71 earned-run average in their final season?

"I had that record with the Royals in '72," says Ted. "Eleven earned runs in forty-five appearances. And they sent me a contract for 1973 with a 20 percent pay cut. I called Cedric Tallis, the general manager, and said, 'What's this? If you don't want me, please do me a favor and release me so I can hook on with another team.' But he didn't, at least not until February 8, and by then it was too late to get a job. And that's how it ended for me. I never even made it to spring training for one last shot."

If the end was sudden, the memories of the good years are warm ones. Ted thinks most fondly of his years with the Cubs.

"Oh, they treated you right," he says. "More like a human being than anyone else. If you had a good year, they took care of you. No holdouts were necessary. I only met Mr. Wrigley a few times, but he was a super guy."

Ted's first Fireman of the Year award came in 1965 with the Cubs, in his first season in Chicago. He won another one at Cincinnati two years later, in his first season with the Reds. Both plaques hang in his Gastonia, North Carolina, home, where he also proudly displays the baseball from his first major league victory, recorded in 1955 while with the Washington Senators.

"Russ Kemmerer, a teammate, painted the ball with the date, and the words 'Ted's 1st big league win.' "

Ted's closest chance at a World Series ring came with the 1969 Cubs, but they were beaten out by the Mets. "I think Leo Durocher would have fared better if he'd rested a few of the players," recalls Ted, "but still, he was quite a

guy himself. Memorable. He could chew you out one minute, and the next thing you knew he was taking you out to
dinner."

It was in the 1960s that saves became the important statistic they are are today, and Abernathy was among the first
to put up big numbers there. He had thirty-one saves in
1965 and twenty-eight in 1967, when his ERA was 1.27,
allowing only fifteen earned runs in 106 innings.

"When I left baseball, I tried for five years to get back in
as a pitching coach," he says. "But nothing developed. It
was probably because with my unorthodox delivery, they
thought I couldn't teach pitching. But one day in 1980, I was
visiting my son in Baltimore and we went to Memorial Stadium to see the Royals play the Orioles.

"Jim Frey, who was managing the Royals, asked me to
stop by the clubhouse and speak to a young reliever named
Dan Quisenberry about throwing sidearm. I don't know if it
was a big help," says Ted with a grin, "but I think he makes
about two million dollars a year now."

When no coaching offers materialized, Ted took a job with
Summay Building Systems in Dallas, North Carolina, about
seven miles from his home.

"I'm a receiving man," he explains. "We build modular
homes and sell them. I've been with the company for fourteen years now. I've got my health, and I'm even a little
lighter than when I pitched. Sometimes you read about old
teammates with heart problems, or other health problems,
and it gives you pause."

Ted's best friend from his playing days are former Royals'
teammates Bobby Knoop and Bruce Dal Canton, and he has
a friendship with a Gastonia native of another era, Buddy
Lewis, who played for the Senators in the 1930s and 1940s.

"Buddy and I were of different generations, but having

both been Senators, and both from Gastonia, we have a common bond. You don't run into that many Senators anymore. Or maybe not that many who'll confess to it."

As a postscript, Ted adds, "I still love baseball. I still try and get to Atlanta at least once a year just to see a game in person. But kids today, I don't know. A few years ago I coached a junior team, and you had to worry about them just showing up for the games."

Cleveland Indians

MAX ALVIS

BORN 1938
MINOR LEAGUES 1959–62
INDIANS 1962–69
BREWERS 1970

---

*I*n the early 1960s, when the American League was just beginning to lose all of those All-Star Games, you wouldn't know it by the caliber of their third basemen. If anything, it was something of a golden age at the position, with almost each team claiming an all-star-type man at the "hot corner."

There were Brooks Robinson (Baltimore), Clete Boyer (New York), Frank Malzone (Boston), Ed Charles (Kansas City), Pete Ward (Chicago), Rich Rollins (Minnesota), Don Wert (Detroit), and in the vest-style uniform of the Cleveland Indians, Roy Maxwell Alvis—"Max" for short.

Max had a .274 rookie season in 1963 with twenty-two home runs, and the most putouts in the league among third basemen. There were some who thought Max might emerge from the pack as the best after Robinson.

But while the life of an athlete is always precarious and an injury could come at any time, the unexpected illness that has nothing to do with baseball is also out there, lingering as a possibility at all times. A few weeks before the 1964 All-Star Game, Max suffered an attack of spinal meningitis, a serious if not career-ending illness.

"It happened so suddenly," he recalls, speaking from his office in Jasper, Texas. "We had arrived in Boston to play the Red Sox, and it hit."

While it could have ended his career, Max responded well to medical care, and in fact surprised most observers by returning to the Indians' lineup in August. The team, which had gotten off well, had played poorly during his absence.

"It was just not meant to be for us that season," he says. "We had some good players—Leon Wagner, Johnny Romano, Sam McDowell, Don McMahon—but Birdie Tebbetts had a heart attack; the whole year got off poorly."

Not only was Max's return a surprise, but also he wound up with a respectable season, hitting eighteen home runs. The following year he played in his first of two All-Star Games, twice more did he better twenty home runs, and he led all the league's third basemen in putouts in 1965, 1966, and 1967. This, of course, was at a time when Brooks Robinson was coming off his MVP season in Baltimore.

"Don't let the statistics fool you," says Max. "I really was never the same player after the illness. I was never as strong as before I got sick. But I'm happy there were not lasting effects, and I'm fine today. I weighed 185 as a player, and I weigh 187 today," he says with a chuckle, pointing out that "it's somewhat redistributed."

Max had begun learning the insurance business while still playing for the Indians. He spent his final campaign with the all-new Milwaukee Brewers in 1970, then retired to enter the general insurance business in his hometown of Jasper. Seven years later he went to work for the First National Bank of Jasper and today is an executive vice president, essentially working as a loan officer.

"These are tough times in Texas," he explains. "The economy has been tough, and there are times my job can get really unpleasant. Basically, in times like these, the loan demand is down, and there are more and more collection problems with existing loans. That's where foreclosure can come in, and that's certainly the unpleasant part of all of this."

Jasper is about 135 miles from Houston, and Max is generally out of touch with major league baseball today. "We're isolated here," he says. "I do run into former players at an occasional golf tournament, or an Old Timers' Game. But my younger son, David, a first baseman, is in the Indians' system now, so I'm reliving my youth through him. At this point, however, he's not yet had the kind of year that would get anyone's attention. But we're obviously hoping he makes it."

"If I have a rooting interest in baseball at all, it's been rekindled by David. I'm still an Indians fan, but you get wrapped up in other careers, family. And, say, it's been seventeen years, hasn't it?"

Los Angeles Dodgers

SANDY AMOROS

BORN 1930
MINOR LEAGUES 1952–54,
  1958–59
DODGERS 1952, 1954–57,
  1959–60
TIGERS 1960
MINOR LEAGUES 1961–62

*W*hen the weather turns cool each October, cool enough so that it becomes necessary to wear a sweater during Florida evenings, Sandy Amoros' thoughts return to the vastness of left field in Yankee Stadium. It's game seven of the 1955 World Series. He is racing to the foul pole to snare an impossible-to-grab drive off the bat of Yogi Berra. The motion becomes frozen into a photograph, one Sandy has seen thousands of times.

"I think about that moment a lot," he says in Spanish,

"especially around World Series time. Sometimes they play it on television this time of year."

In 1985 the Dodgers invited all the members of that 1955 world championship club to Vero Beach, Florida, for a thirtieth reunion. It wasn't a long trip for Sandy, who now lives in Tampa, but it was a long journey back in time.

"My last year in the major leagues was 1960," he says. "Then I went back to play at Denver in the minors, and in 1962 I played for the Mexico City Reds. But my family was still in Cuba, so I went back when my career ended. Once you returned, it was difficult to leave again. Finally, in 1967, I was able to leave with my entire family, and the Dodgers were nice enough to invite me out to Los Angeles because I needed seven more days on the team to qualify for a better pension. They made me a coach and I got the needed days. They are a wonderful organization, always doing things like that."

Sandy was a lifetime .255 hitter who topped a hundred games only three times. He is not among the first names people recall when thinking of the "Boys of Summer." But New York held a special place for him, and that was the scene of his greatest triumphs.

"I went back to the Bronx," he recalls, "I got an apartment, and I took a job with the Parks Department. I worked on the New York City baseball program, caring for the ball fields. It was okay. It was New York and fans knew my name. They made me feel special."

He then worked for an electrical equipment supply company, but a bad case of arthritis caused him to retire and move to Florida for the better climate. He moved into the Cuban section of Miami for a year, then took his family west, to Tampa.

To baseball fans, Sandy would drop in and out of sight.

He would occasionally make a Dodger old timers' gathering and then might disappear for some years without being heard from.

"I live in a Hispanic community here," he says, "and there are a lot of baseball fans who know me either from Brooklyn, Cuba, or winter baseball. I like the recognition. I like talking baseball."

Separated from his wife, he lives alone in a Tampa apartment. His life has become more difficult, for just three weeks before this conversation, he had a leg amputated. A severe infection in his toes caused doctors to fear that a case of gangrene was possible.

"I'm very optimistic about my life," he says. "I have two daughters and four grandchildren—fourteen, twelve, nine, and two. I look forward to living a long life for my grandchildren."

Sandy enjoys watching baseball on television and wonders if he'll ever see anyone who quite reminds him of himself.

"There aren't too many players five-seven anymore," he observes, "especially not outfielders. And it sure is rare when you see a play like that catch I got off Yogi."

LOU BERBERET

BORN 1929
MINOR LEAGUES 1950,
  1953–55
YANKEES 1954–55
SENATORS 1956–58
RED SOX 1958
TIGERS 1959–60

*L*ike many before and after him, Lou Berberet was a catcher in the Yankee minor league system who had the task of displacing Yogi Berra, Elston Howard, or Johnny Blanchard on the roster. Forget it.

Signed by the Yankees in 1950, he spent four seasons in the organization, save for two in the military, and even got into a total of seven games for New York in 1954 and 1955. But then, just before spring training of 1956, he was dealt to the Washington Senators to begin a five-year career as a journeyman catcher and to taste the good life of big-league baseball.

He chuckles now to think of his career, and says, "All my managers were always on my butt about my weight. I weighed about 210 as a player, and they all thought I should have been around 195. I guess I should have listened to them. Maybe I'd have hit .240."

There's good humor in his voice as he says he got out of the game in time to protect his lifetime .230 average.

While he acknowledged that it would have been nice to have been part of the Yankee championship teams of the 1950s, he knows he was not alone in finding the road to glory blocked by the presence of Berra, Howard, and Blanchard.

"Gus Triandos, Sherm Lollar, Clint Courtney, myself, at one time . . . half the American League had catchers developed in the Yankee system. Then there was Ralph Houk; he didn't get traded, but he became a coach and then the manager. And he was a good receiver, too."

Lou played for the Washington Senators in 1956 and 1957. He spent most of the 1958 season with the Boston Red Sox, where Jackie Jensen won MVP honors and Ted Williams won the batting title at age forty. Then he spent his last two seasons, 1959 and 1960, with the Detroit Tigers, the team he most closely associates himself with today.

"That's funny, to think of myself with them the most, but in '59 I had my most playing time in the majors [a hundred games] and caught opposite that good pitching staff of Jim Bunning, Paul Foytack, Don Mossi, and Frank Lary. Now, of course, Sparky Anderson manages over there. We were roommates in winter ball in Venezuela, so you could say I have a rooting interest.

"But I have a stronger rooting interest in the Cardinals, because I played with Whitey Herzog in the Yankee system and we were traded together to the Senators and were good friends."

During Lou's career he did some delivery work in off-seasons for a liquor distributor and worked in a warehouse. Nothing glamorous, certainly. When he didn't get a contract for 1961, even with expansion, he returned to his hometown of Long Beach, California, and worked as a sales manager and general manager for his cousin's liquor business for seven years. You can also find him in the 1964 *Official Baseball Guide* as the assistant coach of the '63 American Legion champions.

In 1976 Lou moved to Las Vegas and became a general manager for Nevada Liquor Company. He is married for the second time and has five daughters and a son.

In Vegas he bumps into old colleagues like Herzog, Mickey Mantle, and Billy Martin.

"I've got a nice collection of autographed balls," he interjects. "I've got one signed by Vice-President Nixon from my Senator days. I have the first shutout I ever caught—Camilo Pascual gave it to me, even though the pitcher usually keeps those things. I guess he knew he'd get a lot more. With me it wasn't a sure thing.

"I've got my first home run ball, and one I hit when I was with Toronto in 1955 that I hit a ton. I also have that big book with all the Topps baseball cards in it—which includes a few of mine."

At fifty-eight, with a diabetic condition under control and with his humor intact, Lou is a delightful bearer of good memories from 1950s baseball.

Detroit Tigers

RENO BERTOIA

BORN 1935
TIGERS 1953–58
MINOR LEAGUES 1956
SENATORS 1959–60
TWINS 1961
ATHLETICS 1961
TIGERS 1961–62
MINOR LEAGUES 1963

---

*R*eno Bertoia, with one of baseball's most lyrical names, was born in St. Vito Udine, Italy, but moved to Windsor, Ontario, with his family when he was only twenty-two months old. He still lives there today.

He was a ten-thousand-dollar bonus baby with the Tigers, and a major leaguer at eighteen.

"Oh, that was a lot of money back then," he says with a sigh. "We gave a thousand dollars of it to my mother so that she could make a visit back to Italy. But I'll tell you, with the benefit of hindsight, it was such a poor rule for baseball, forcing bonus players to stay in the majors. What a waste for everyone. I was so shy at eighteen, just not ready for it all. How I wish I could have been more assertive and aggressive back then."

He may have been shy, but he was not without a sense of history. He still has the ball with which he recorded his first spring-training hit, and the ball that produced his first regular-season hit.

"They were both," he says proudly, "home runs."

Not until 1956 did Reno finally go to the minors for that needed playing time and experience. It seemed to pay dividends, for he returned to the Tigers in 1957 and got off quickly with the bat.

"One other thing I still have today, framed and displayed," he adds, "is a newspaper clipping showing the American League batting leaders in May 1957. I'm on top with a .390 average, and some guy named Ted Williams is second."

Bertoia knows he was never a star, but his memories are precious, perhaps because of that.

"I was with the Senators one time, and we were playing in Detroit," he explains. "So my family came out to see me play. On the Saturday of the series, I made a bad play at third, and after that inning, I was pinch-hit for. I was very embarrassed by that.

"The next day we had a doubleheader and I had the winning hits in both games. After the game, my dad came downstairs and he was crying. He told me he had prayed for me the night after the error. I'll never forget that experience."

Reno's father, at eighty-six, is a far more avid baseball fan today than his son is. Reno is on to another career.

"After I finished playing in 1964, I went to Japan. But my wife was pregnant, and it just didn't work out. I left after two months.

"I returned to Windsor and worked as a teacher at Corpus Christi High School for two years, then moved here to Assumption High, where I've been since 1966. I'm the head of the history department."

Asked whether baseball plays any part in his life, he smiles. "Oh, there are times one of my students comes in and says, 'My dad said you did such and such in baseball. Is this true?' And, of course, it's a nice thing to be identified with."

Reno went through a divorce not long ago, something he describes as "difficult for me," but he has great pride in his three children. "My son, Carl, is studying for his Ph.D. in sociology; my daughter Ruth is a teacher; and my daughter Gina just went off to Toronto, where she's hoping to become an actress."

In recent years, Bertoia has been drawn back to the Tigers' organization through the efforts of Tom Monaghan, the owner. "He's just been great at establishing an alumni group among the Tigers, and I'm secretary of the organization. He lets us sit in the owner's box, which is some treat for my father, let me tell you. And it's great to see some of the old guys like Kaline, Hoeft, and Foytack. I'm glad to be part of this outfit, really."

EWELL BLACKWELL

BORN 1922
MINOR LEAGUES 1942
REDS 1942, 1946–52
YANKEES 1952–53
MINOR LEAGUES 1954
ATHLETICS 1955

*A*sk just about any hitter, particularly a right-handed one, who played in the late 1940s and early 1950s who their toughest opponent was, and the name you'll most likely hear is Ewell "The Whip" Blackwell.

Indeed, Blackwell pitched in five consecutive All-Star Games between 1947 and 1951 and didn't allow a single run in eleven innings.

At six-five and 195 pounds, Blackwell threw with a three-quarter delivery that positively baffled hitters. He had a reputation as a fearsome pitcher, unafraid to knock a hitter down.

He was discovered by the Reds in San Dimas, California, in 1939 when only a high school junior. He was signed in 1942 and by the end of the season was in the majors. After World War II service in General George Patton's army, he returned in 1946 to go 9–13 before his spectacular 1947 season.

Yet for fans under forty, his name is almost unknown, and most certainly there is no mental picture at all of his intimidating delivery. For someone who seemed destined for the Hall of Fame, his current fame is almost nil.

Part of this, no doubt, comes from an almost hermitlike posture when it comes to baseball. And part of it, of course, comes from his rapid demise after 1951. The twenty-two-game winner of 1947 was only 82–78 lifetime.

"I'm not bitter," he says in response to a question. But when pressed, he admits to never attending old timers' gatherings, turning down requests to appear at card conventions and autograph sessions, and especially not doing any interviews.

"Too many of them don't come out right," he says. "I've learned not to do them. You never get quoted accurately."

While he couldn't cite the particular article in question, it was apparent that something had burned him along the way.

He only watches baseball "once in a while," and he laughs with sarcasm when asked about the state of baseball today.

"These pitchers today," he says, "it's a bad thing. You're supposed to finish games. Starting pitchers are supposed to finish. Too many changes."

Blackwell himself finished 69 of 169 starts in the big leagues, but that 1947 season set a standard for him that he never recaptured. It was his second full season with the Reds. He was 22–8, completing twenty-three of his thirty-three starts. He won sixteen consecutive games, led the league with 193 strikeouts, and came the closest any man has ever come to matching Johnny Vander Meer's feat of two consecutive no-hitters.

On June 18, 1947, Blackwell no-hit the Boston Braves. In his next start, he pitched eight innings of no-hit ball before allowing a ground-ball single by Eddie Stanky of the Dodgers. Rookie Jackie Robinson followed with a single, but then Blackwell retired the next three batters for a two-hit shutout. Ironically, Vander Meer's second no-hitter was against Brooklyn, and he was a teammate of Blackwell's when he saw his nine-year-old record challenged.

But he lost the magic and was only 51–57 for the rest of his major-league career. He started a game for the Yankees in the 1952 World Series against Brooklyn but was only a shadow of his former self. Some said he never was the same after a kidney stone attack.

After his career, he took a job as South Carolina manager of a large distillery ("but don't mention their name—they don't deserve the publicity"). He later worked as a security guard and retired in 1983. He and his wife, Dottie, have four grandchildren, too young to appreciate their once-celebrated grandfather's accomplishments.

Although a member of the Cincinnati Reds' Hall of Fame, Blackwell thinks the Cooperstown version is "all politics, all who you know."

He keeps in touch with a few old teammates, mostly Grady Hatton, and claims to have "some souvenirs" from his playing days and to have "turned down offers in baseball."

Blackwell moved his family to Transylvania County, North Carolina, in 1975, claiming, "we like the quiet, restful atmosphere, and that's the way we'd like to keep it." It appears he has succeeded, for twelve years later, he seemed as much out of touch with his own place in history as the baseball world was out of touch with him. He seemed remarkably unaware of the awe in which his former opponents hold him, yet not at all bothered by the thought that he was somehow missing accolades and cheers.

Ron Blomberg

BORN 1948
MINOR LEAGUES 1967–71
YANKEES 1969, 1971–77
WHITE SOX 1978

*R*on Blomberg, baseball's first designated hitter, still thinks it's a great rule. "It adds more hitting—people like to see hitting, not automatic outs," he says.

Retired since 1978 and living in his hometown of Atlanta, Blomberg did indeed have a gift at the plate. Give him a fastball from a right-handed pitcher and he could mash it. He was less successful under other circumstances but still had a .293 career average, and in 1973 was batting over .400 as late as July 4 and made the covers of *Sports Illustrated* and *The Sporting News*.

"Not long ago, there was a chart in *Baseball Digest,*" he says, "showing the top ten Yankee hitters of all time. There I was, ninth, at .302, right in there with Ruth and Gehrig and DiMaggio. Couldn't believe it."

"It hurts to think about my career," he confesses. "I was injured a lot and was never the same after I wrecked my shoulder crashing into the concrete wall in Winter Haven during spring training. I'm thirty-eight—I could still be playing . . . there was always all that talk about all the potential. . . ." His voice drops off.

Blomberg recalls his historic at-bat as the first DH well. "Of course, we'd been using the DH in spring training, so it wasn't startling. Jim Ray Hart and I were going to platoon at DH that first year, and since we opened in Fenway Park and Luis Tiant was pitching, I was in the lineup. As for being first, it was just the luck of being in the Eastern Time Zone for a day game, starting ahead of anyone else, and batting in the top of the first. The Red Sox' DH was Orlando Cepeda, and if I hadn't batted in the first, it would have been him in the last of the first. When I came up, the PA announcer [Sherm Feller] made a special announcement about baseball history being made, but the people didn't know whether they were supposed to cheer or not, since I was a Yankee. Anyway, I walked, and after the game, the bat was sent to Cooperstown. Funny to have a bat there commemorating a walk."

At the end of the '73 season, Yankee Stadium was remodeled, and Blomberg managed to salvage part of the auxiliary scoreboard from right-center field, where the numbers would be lit after each inning. "It's about eight feet long—we got a truck to haul it away," he says.

Playing for the Yankees was special for a Jewish athlete. The day he was the nation's number one draft choice in

1967, they had a press conference in Yankee Stadium, and Ron did his first one-on-one interview with Walter Cronkite, who was at the ball park to take in the game and interview the "Jewish Yankee" for CBS News.

"New York fans were the greatest in the world. Most of my fan mail still comes from there, and they are still great to me there," he says. "I hated to leave New York but I had been hurt for two years and needed to try my luck somewhere else. I needed a new scene."

He became a free agent and signed with the White Sox. "Bill Veeck was a super guy, and I homered in my first game, but there wasn't much after that. I was released after one year and got paid off in full for the next season. I was the first player that happened to."

Today, balding but in excellent shape, Ron is the co-owner of a successful career counseling business, USA Career Management, in Atlanta. He has eighteen employees and fits easily into the business world.

"I've never even been to Atlanta Stadium," he says. "I'd have nothing to say to the players. I was a player; I was never really a fan."

He and his second wife, Beth, have a baby daughter named Chesley. His son Adam, from his first wife, lives in Florida and plays Little League. "Adam never really remembers me as a player—I'd love to get some old tapes to show him, but they didn't save much, even in the seventies," he says with regret.

IIe had a happy-go-lucky reputation as a player, and many would be surprised to find him successful in business. But he made the switch, and you can find him behind *The Wall Street Journal* more often now than *The Sporting News*.

Left to right
—Whitey Lockman and Bob Boyd

BOB BOYD

BORN 1926
MINOR LEAGUES 1950–55
WHITE SOX 1951, 1953–54
ORIOLES 1956–60
ATHLETICS 1961
BRAVES 1961

*T*hey called him "Ropes," because he was seemingly born to hit line drives. Bob Boyd, a lifetime major-league .293 hitter between 1951 and 1961, was mostly with the White Sox and Orioles. Four times he batted over .300 in the majors.

"I played three or four years in the old Negro Leagues before I was signed by the White Sox," he recalls from his home in Wichita, Kansas. "So I was one of the first black players in the majors, although by 1951 it wasn't really big news anymore."

"I was born in 1926," says Boyd, "not 1925, like some said. But whether they thought I was thirty-five or thirty-six at the end, I knew it was over. I got an ulcer in my last years, and no matter what I did, I just couldn't get over it. I used to have to call time out when I was in the field, run into the dugout, and throw up. It was no way to play ball."

It got to him in his final year in Baltimore, 1960, when the "Baby Birds" of Paul Richards were challenging the Yankees for the pennant. Jim Gentile had taken Boyd's job at first base, and so in 1961 Boyd went to Kansas City, and then to Milwaukee, where he finished up the season. But the ulcer had really finished him.

"Funny thing was," he recalls, "when I was done, I got an offer to go to Wichita to play semipro ball. Wichita was the top spot in the country for semipro, and I was on a team with a lot of ex-big leaguers. Pat Gillick, who's the GM in Toronto now, was also a player on that team. We were real good, and my ulcer went away, too! Can't tell you why, but it never bothered me again."

In Wichita, Boyd also worked for the city bus company, part of the deal for getting paid to play ball. For twenty years he drove a city bus in Wichita, and for a lot of them he continued to be a fixture on the local ball fields.

"It was nice . . . everyone knew me in Wichita. There were always stories in the papers, people would talk to me on the bus. It was a good life."

As with many players, Bob gets more mail today than he ever did. The hobbies of collecting cards or autographs have grown enormously in recent years, and many fans—children and adults—seem determined to get complete collections, even among players they never heard of. A few of Bob's letters recall his prowess at hitting line drives. A few remarked at the Orioles' good fortune to have had so few first basemen in their history—Boyd, Jim Gentile, Boog Powell, and Eddie Murray. But some seem quite unfamiliar with Bob and just ask that he sign the enclosed card and return it in the self-addressed envelope. He satisfies all comers.

He lives well, with his wife, Valca, who works for Coleman, the outdoor equipment company, in Wichita. Bob is retired, in good health, and goes to Kansas City often, where he stays in the visiting team's hotel and watches the Royals.

"I can't understand all these home runs this year," he said in 1987. "I can't wait to play in an Old Timers' Day and see if I can hit one out."

Bob only hit nineteen in his major-league career, however, so it seems unlikely.

"The Orioles were a great bunch of guys," he says, "especially Brooks Robinson. And Paul Richards, my manager, was a very smart baseball man. He had me in Chicago first, then traded to get me over to Baltimore."

Boyd mentions with fondness a recent baseball card show in Wichita attended by Brooks, Willie Stargell, Mickey Mantle, and others. "Mickey made a speech about what a good hitter I was that made me feel great," he says.

Boyd's top major-league salary was $18,500. "I'd be happy to play for the meal money today," he says, then chuckles and adds, "I think I could still play, too."

BILLY BRUTON

BORN 1929
MINOR LEAGUES 1950–52
BRAVES 1953–60
TIGERS 1961–64

---

*N*early thirty-five years after his major-league debut, Billy Bruton still calls his rookie season the most memorable of his life.

"Oh, yes, 1953, that was great," he says from his home in Detroit. "It was the first year the Braves were in Milwaukee, but I had played there in '52 when it was a minor-league club. So even though I was a rookie, I was familiar to the fans, and in a way, all the players from Boston were the new guys. I was treated really well.

"I played 151 games as a rookie, something I'm very proud

of, and I had great support from my teammates. There were
no jealousies on the Braves, none at all. When you joined
the club, you were there to help as a member of the team.
None of us were there for individual glory. And I think that's
what helped us become successful there."

Successful they were. After just missing the 1956 pennant, the Braves won in 1957 and 1958, and just missed
again in 1959. Bruton led the National League in stolen bases
in each of his first three seasons, with twenty-six, thirty-
four, and twenty-five, respectively.

"I guess that doesn't sound like much today," he says
with a laugh, "but we played a different style of baseball in
the fifties. We only stole bases when it meant something for
the team, not just for personal gain.

"When I went to the Tigers in 1961, I discovered that
the American League ran even less than we did. Except for
Luis Aparicio, I guess. But in the National League, we would
steal more bases and use the squeeze play more. Maybe it
all came down from when John McGraw managed the Giants,
or so I used to hear. The American League would find guys
on first base and they'd wait to be driven in from there."

Bruton enjoys watching baseball today, but gets frustrated watching the younger players make mistakes.

"In my day," he says, "when you got to the big leagues,
you were a major leaguer. Now it seems like the players
hardly stay in the minors more than two years. We played
a sounder game fundamentally. I played aggressively and
conscientiously. I was intent on achieving perfection. There
are only two players I see today who bring that to mind:
Ozzie Smith and Pete Rose."

Bruton retired in Detroit, where he played the last four
seasons of his career. He has worked for Chrysler for
twenty-two years, currently in the Customer Service Department.

His wife is the daughter of Hall of Famer Judy Johnson. They have four children, one of whom still lives at home, and eight grandchildren. And he'll talk baseball with anyone who wants to listen.

"In my time, when we traveled by train, we talked baseball constantly. In '61, when expansion came, we'd fly around the country, and you lost a lot of baseball talk. We'd fly by night and try to sleep on the planes. Train travel was more conducive to day trips and relaxation. You'd get to your next town better rested.

"We had a reunion in Atlanta in 1982 for the 1957 Braves. I was hurt that year and didn't play in the World Series, but it was pretty much the same as the '58 club, and I hit .412 in that Series. It was great to see my old teammates, including a couple I hadn't seen in more than twenty years: Bob Hazel and Mel Roach."

Billy gets to four or five Tigers games each year and usually is recognized immediately by the older Detroit fans. He enjoys the attention, and he roots as strongly for the Tigers as he does for the Braves.

Only ten pounds over his trim playing weight and in fine health, Billy, at fifty-eight, gives the impression of remaining the consummate professional—the sort of guy Lee Iacocoa must have in mind when he sings the praises of Chrysler people.

JOHNNY CALLISON

BORN 1939
MINOR LEAGUES 1957–59
WHITE SOX 1958–59
PHILLIES 1960–69
CUBS 1970–71
YANKEES 1972–73

*T*he next time you see a bartender at Vinny's in Huntington Valley, Pennsylvania, who reminds you of television's Sam Malone of *Cheers,* take another look. This time it *is* a former big-league star, and his name is Johnny Callison, a big hero in Philadelphia who almost won the 1964 MVP award.

"Everyone comes in and talks baseball. We have a good time," says Johnny, who seems to welcome times that put a smile on his face.

In July 1986, John was felled by a hemorrhaging ulcer. He

passed out and was rushed to surgery, where half his stomach was removed and he had a quintuple-bypass operation. He lost twenty pounds and took half a year to recover.

"Thank God I kept my baseball medical insurance," he says. "It was the one good thing I did."

Callison's health setback was the latest in a string that had haunted him since his playing career ended in 1973.

"I thought I'd try to hang on another year or two," he recalls, "and I called a few clubs, but nothing came of it. So I got out. And once you're out, you're out. It's very hard to get back in. I didn't want to go back to the minors as a coach, and in the majors, they seem to have an image of coaches as being utility infielders or something. If you hit a little, they think you can't coach."

So Johnny went home to Glenside, Pennsylvania, near the town of his greatest heroics, Philadelphia. He sold electronics, did some public relations, and sold cars.

"They were hard times," he says. "It probably hurt my ulcer. I'd grab at almost anything."

"I finally retired when I hit forty-five and could collect my pension. Thank God for that and for the medical insurance."

Johnny is best remembered for his game-winning home run in the 1964 All-Star Game at Shea Stadium. The ball was retrieved by Rocky Colavito, who gave it to Jim Bunning as a souvenir. Bunning eventually gave it to Callison, and it's his prize memento now.

"I gave a lot of stuff away," he says, "until my kids finally told me to stop."

Another prize that could have been his was the 1964 MVP award. It seemed like a lock for Callison that year, as he led the Phillies with 104 RBIs and hit 31 homers for what seemed like a pennant-bound season. But the Phillies collapsed, blew the pennant in the final week to St. Louis, and the MVP award went to the Cardinals' Ken Boyer, with Callison finishing second.

"I hit okay that last week; I was hot, in fact. I hit four or five homers, three in one game. But we lost that game, 14–8. Nothing was going right. We were there. We missed it.

"I was a kid with the 1959 White Sox. I wasn't eligible for the World Series, so I didn't attend it, but I was on that team for a little while. Little did I know that would be my only shot at a Series. I wish I'd played in one.

"I was traded by the White Sox when I was twenty. Do you know what it means to be traded at twenty? I thought I was finished. I liked the White Sox, although I guess it would have been tough to have played in Comiskey Park. Not a good power ball park."

A few years ago, a friend offered Johnny a job to help tend bar at Vinny's.

"I went to bartenders' school, and now I work there four days a week. I had some pictures up at first, but now everyone knows who I am."

John has three daughters, and each of them has two daughters. "Our dog's a girl, too," he says with a smile. "It's just me and my wife at home now. It's great."

He says it's great, but there's a tinge in his voice that lets you know he felt there could have been a niche for him somewhere in baseball.

New York Yankees

BOB CERV

BORN 1926
MINOR LEAGUES 1950–53
YANKEES 1951–56
ATHLETICS 1957–60
YANKEES 1960
ANGELS 1961
YANKEES 1961–62
COLT .45'S 1962

---

*B*eing out of professional baseball for a quarter of a century has done nothing to diminish Bob Cerv's interest in the current state of the game.

He is as interested in the fates and fortunes of Craig McMurtry and Mike Moore as he is fond of his memories of Roger Maris and Mickey Mantle.

McMurtry and Moore are two of the "several dozen" players Cerv coached in semipro ball during summers in Kansas. Maris and Mantle were his roommates during the glorious summer of 1961 when they hit 115 home runs. With

Cerv, the trio's Queens apartment accounted for 121 of the team's 240 home runs.

Bob is chiefly remembered as a valuable member of the Yankees' bench strength during three tours of duty with the Bronx Bombers (1951–56, 1960, and 1961–62). But it was in Kansas City, between 1957 and 1960, that he had a chance to play regularly and show what he could do.

In those three seasons as a regular, he hit sixty-nine home runs and drove in 235 runs for weak clubs. His thirty-eight homers in 1958 as well as his 305 total bases and .592 slugging percentage will forever be listed as the all-time Kansas City A's records as long as the record books are kind enough to list defunct teams.

"I suppose I'll always think of myself as a Yankee," says Cerv, now sixty-one. "But I got a lot of self-satisfaction in Kansas City. I was able to show myself what I could do if I'd been a regular throughout my career.

Bob was a big man in Kansas City. Not only was he a native of the Midwest, born in Weston, Nebraska, but also he played minor-league ball in Kansas City starting in 1950, following his graduation from the University of Nebraska. There he earned a teaching degree, which he was able to put to good use after his playing days ended with the Houston Colt .45's in their maiden season of 1962.

He became a college coach and teacher at John F. Kennedy University in Nebraska, where he spent ten years before moving on to Sioux Empire College in Iowa for similar dual roles. In the summers he would travel to Liberal, Kansas, to coach outstanding semipro teams. Out of those teams came such names as Ron Guidry, Steve Rogers, Phil Garner, Rick Honeycutt, Doug Drabek, Calvin Schiraldi, Jim Acker, and the aforementioned McMurtry and Moore. When he picks up a newspaper today, his eyes scan the box scores for the players he coached, rather than for his former teams.

In 1984 he retired from coaching when he had a hip replacement. Part of his rehabilitation was to do a lot of walking. "As long as I had to walk, I got myself a metal detector and took up coin collecting," he says with a chuckle. "I've picked up about fifteen thousand coins and rings in the last three years—no kidding. It's amazing how much money people drop. And the pre-1964 stuff has silver in it."

His recent coaching has kept him good-humored and anything but a sour old timer who thinks baseball stopped being good when he retired. "But," he notes, "today's major leaguers are still learning when they're in the majors. You see so many mistakes, so many players throwing to the wrong base and so forth. It's probably because they don't spend enough time in the minors. And the strike zone today—it's as wide as it is high. I actually feel sorry for the pitchers."

Bob and his wife, Phyllis, raised ten children, all of whom graduated from college and only one of whom still lives at home, in Lincoln, Nebraska. One of his three sons was a West Point graduate.

He attends card shows on occasion ("My grandson gets these journals that show the prices of things—it's hard to believe"), but he has pretty much given up going to Old Timers' Days since clubs stopped paying for wives to accompany their husbands. He kept in close touch with his old friend Roger Maris right until Roger's death but has pretty much lost touch with his other teammates. He's got cartons of old equipment, bats, and an old gray Yankee uniform, gets *Yankee Magazine* in the mail, and watches the CNN sports updates to keep current.

"I've also got about a dozen autographed baseballs from

the 1958 All-Star Game," he adds, the game in which the starting American League outfield was Mickey Mantle, Jackie Jensen, and Cerv. Ted Williams, that year's batting champ, was on the bench. "I could probably put another kid through college on those baseballs."

CHRIS CHAMBLISS

BORN 1948
MINOR LEAGUES 1970
INDIANS 1971–74
YANKEES 1974–79
BRAVES 1980–86

*N*ot many people can claim to have had three successful stints in three different cities, but Chris Chambliss was a popular star in Cleveland, New York, and Atlanta between 1971 and 1986.

In Cleveland he succeeded the popular Hawk Harrelson at first base and won the American League Rookie of the Year award after only 118 minor-league games. In New York he played for three consecutive pennant winners and hit the last-of-the-ninth home run to win the 1976 pennant in the final game of the League Championship Series against Kan-

sas City. In Atlanta he played for the 1982 division champions and moved into the $750,000 salary range. But after
batting .311 in his final year, mostly as a pinch-hitter, his
contract ran out and no one called with a job, not even an
American League club in need of a DH.

"I couldn't get an invitation," he reflects from his north-
ern New Jersey home. "It was disappointing. I stayed in
shape, and there was always hope, but the phone just didn't
ring. By the middle of the summer of 1987, it pretty much
settled in that no one was going to call.

"These have been pretty quiet days. But I won't sit at
home. I'm hoping to get into the securities business, and
these last few weeks, I've been going to Wall Street. But I
haven't gotten a position there yet either."

Chambliss disputes the fact that today's players are all so
rich they never have to work after their careers are over.

"In the first place, you're too young to sit home—you still
want to work. In addition, you don't exactly get a big lump
of money like the newspapers say. Most players defer the
money over a number of years. Then you invest in tax shel-
ters and things, but of course you never really see that
money. And naturally, you've adjusted your expenses up-
ward and hope to be able to continue living that way. You
get to a certain level and want to maintain it. You might
think I'm rich, but I'm not."

Around the house, Chambliss has a lot to remind himself
of his glory days, which he says belong with the Yankees.
"That's where I got to play in World Series, and that's where
people I was involved with still work—like Steinbrenner,
Piniella, and so on."

Chris worked for George Steinbrenner and Ted Turner,
two of baseball's more colorful owners. "In New York,
George is really the city guy, coat and tie every day, and

although you call him George, you think of him as Mr. Steinbrenner. Turner was more laid back, definitely a 'Ted' type. You wouldn't believe how open he was in the clubhouse. He'd discuss trades with players before he'd make them, tell you all about million-dollar deals he was cooking up.

"But he was more involved with his television station. I'll tell you, it was great to play for the Braves and be on the superstation. I'd get letters from Hawaii, Japan, all over."

Although his career was far more than the big home run against Kansas City, his memorabilia include a large framed photo of the moment the ball was hit, and both the bat and the ball from the event.

Did Chris ever touch home plate after the fans poured onto the field?

"Touch home?" he asks. "Listen, third base was gone by the time I got there!"

Told that this book also included Bob Boyd, Chris said, "It's a small world. Bob lives around the corner from my in-laws in Wichita. That's where I broke into pro ball in 1970 and met Audra. When we visit her parents, we always see Bob."

"I might have played out the rest of my career in New York," he adds, "and I would have loved it. But after Thurman Munson was killed, the Yankees had to trade for a catcher, and I was the price. I went to Toronto for Rick Cerone, but they dealt me to Atlanta before spring training. I understood the trade, that's baseball, but I sure wish I had been a free agent instead. It would have been nice to pick my own destiny."

Several weeks after this conversation, Chambliss's telephone finally rang. It was a call from the Yankees, inviting him to return as a front-office official and as a minor-league batting instructor. So it was good-bye, Wall Street, and just as well, for the market crashed several weeks later. The Yankees took him back and made him the team's batting coach, major-league level, for 1988.

HARRY CHITI

BORN 1932
MINOR LEAGUES 1950–52
CUBS 1950–52,
  1955–56
MINOR LEAGUES 1957
ATHLETICS 1958–60
TIGERS 1960–61
METS 1962

---

*I*n Bowie Kuhn's 1987 memoirs he tells a story of crusty old Jim Gallagher, onetime general manager of the Chicago Cubs. Enos Slaughter crashed into Cubs' catcher Harry Chiti, practically knocking him out, but Chiti held onto the ball for the out. The fans roared.

"Some play by Chiti," said Kuhn to Gallagher.

"That's what we pay the S.O.B. for," grumbled Gallagher.

Hearing the story in the living room of his new condo in Bartlett, Tennessee, Chiti smiled. "I don't remember the play," he said, "but I'm sure it was true. You forget a lot of those collisions at the plate. They were pretty common."

Chiti, whose top salary was only $27,000, probably was making around $10,000 when that crash occurred.

Harry joined the Cubs in 1950 after only fifty minor-league games. He was only seventeen at the time, but he didn't register a full major-league season until 1955, after two years in the service.

"As it happened," he explained, "I was in the Army with John Kibler, who became a National League umpire. Kibler had a friend, also in the service, who went on to work for Columbia Motion Pictures. When I got out of baseball [in 1962], I ran into John and he asked me what I'd be doing. I told him I was looking around.

"Well, he introduced me to his buddy, and that led to a job as a district manager for Columbia, going around to the theaters, first in Jacksonville, and later in Dallas, trying to book Columbia movies into their houses. Eventually the process became simplified and was done mostly by telephone. I was laid off in 1970 when they cut back from thirty-two district managers to eleven."

So much for show business.

"By then I was living in Tennessee. My son Dominick had been dating the sheriff's daughter. He knew I'd been a ballplayer, and he knew I was out of work, so he offered me a job in his department. That's how I became a bailiff here in Shelby County. I'd always done a lot of youth work, and he thought it was a good chance to continue working with juveniles. I've been working for the same judge now for ten years."

The people at the court didn't know of Harry's background until some co-workers went to a baseball card show and found some Harry Chiti cards. Now they love talking baseball with him.

Meanwhile, son Dominick, a left-hander, was drafted in the second round by the Orioles in 1976, and while he never reached the majors, he is now a minor-league pitching instructor for Baltimore.

"That keeps me close to the game today," says Harry. "First thing I look at in the morning paper is the sports section, and maybe how Rochester is doing [the Orioles' top farm club]. But I'm pretty much out of touch."

Indeed, heart disease has prevented Harry from attending old timers' gatherings, and the last time the Cubs sent him a questionnaire, he didn't even answer it.

The Cubs dealt him to the Yankee organization after the 1956 season, and while he spent the year at Richmond, not New York, he calls it the most rewarding year of his career.

"With the Cubs, I didn't realize how much there still was to learn. In the one year at Richmond, under manager Ed Lopat, I learned an incredible amount about baseball. The next year, when I was traded to Kansas City, I was at the peak of my game. That Yankee minor league organization was just sensational."

One of his baseball souvenirs comes from his Kansas City days. "In 1960 they played an All-Star Game in K.C., and I was chosen as a bullpen catcher. It wasn't as nice as making the team, but they gave us each a commemorative All-Star cap, and I've still got it."

Chiti's last hurrah came with the fabled 1962 Mets, in their first season, on their way to losing 120 games. Harry caught fourteen games and hit .195.

"It was a bad team, all right," he says. "The problem was only partly the lack of ability. It was also that all of these guys were just thrown together and had no experience playing together. That's important. It's a very difficult situation. But I was only there thirty days or so."

Chiti's New York career ended when he was the player

to be named later in his own trade. He was, in effect, traded for himself. It remains a baseball oddity, such as a quirk in the law that Chiti probably comes across now and then in the Shelby County courtroom.

The next time you're hauled before the judge in Shelby County, you might want to get the bailiff's autograph before paying your fine.

HORACE CLARKE

BORN 1940
MINOR LEAGUES 1958–65
YANKEES 1965–74
PADRES 1974

*I*t wasn't Horace Clarke's fault. Really. It has become fashionable among Yankee fans to recall the dry period of 1965–75—which produced no Yankee pennants—as the "Horace Clarke Era." As it happens, Horace's Yankee career spanned from 1965 to 1974.

Still, just because he had the longevity to play for all those mediocre teams (combined record in his time: 805–804), is that reason to blame it all on him? Is it his fault that the organization could come up with no one better? Should he have resigned in protest?

All of these thoughts bring a smile to his face down in the

Virgin Islands, where he has lived all his life. "The Horace Clarke Era?" he asks. "I suppose it's nice to be remembered at all."

He did disappear into the dust quickly. The Yankees sold him to San Diego midway through the '74 season and replaced him with Sandy Alomar. The team was in Minnesota when Clarke got the news. "I had been in the organization for seventeen years," he notes, "and nobody even shook my hand to say good-bye."

But he can be more proud of his career than some might think. Even his detractors acknowledge that he was a good offensive player. His first two home runs were both grand slams. He had 183 hits in 1969, second in the league to Tony Oliva. He was sixth on the all-time Yankee stolen-base list when he left the club, with a season high of thirty-three. In one amazing month, June 1970, he broke up three no-hitters in the ninth inning—off Joe Niekro, Sonny Siebert and Jim Rooker. That may never happen again.

His best supporters all agree that he may not have been the best double-play man in history. But Clarke led the American League's second baseman in assists in six consecutive seasons, a major-league record. He also led the league in putouts four times, fielding percentage once, and—get this—double plays once. Naturally, part of that had to do with durability, which his critics would say came from protecting himself too much on the pivot. The arguments can still continue.

Frequently the butt of criticism by frustrated sportswriters, Horace can smile softly thinking of them. "It's true, they criticized me, some of them, but here I am living in the beautiful islands, and they are probably still up there pounding the beat."

Speaking in a gentle calypso accent, Clarke was a hero to

young people in the Virgin Islands, and the government quickly employed him in the recreation area after he left baseball. More than a decade later, at forty-seven, he still enjoys working with youngsters.

He told a writer not long ago, "They used to say I couldn't make the double play, that I couldn't field. It hurt me for a long time. It made me think: Was I ever any good? Once I sent for my stats and compared them to other Yankee second basemen. I finally decided I wasn't that bad. I know that after I was gone, some of the sportswriters said I wasn't that bad."

His top salary was forty-two thousand dollars, a little more than half what his double-play partner Gene Michael earned. In their major-league careers Clarke hit .256; Michael, .229.

"He [Michael] was a good negotiator," says Clarke with a chuckle. "One year I asked for a loan to help me out in a real-estate opportunity I was offered. The Yankees told the newspapers that I was 'holding out' for a million dollars. But that's okay. I suppose all is fair in negotiation. They got me for another forty thousand dollars."

Horace is too kind to harbor any bitterness if he thinks he was slighted. He simply recognizes that he was in the wrong place at the wrong time—between Yankee dynasties. But he might also have been "nowhere," never getting his time in the big leagues, never wearing the pinstripes, playing with Mickey Mantle, breaking up three no-hitters in a month.

Most people would be happy to trade places, then go home to beautiful Frederiksted with their wives and children, fish, and coach baseball. Not bad for the bow legged little infielder who wore long-sleeved sweat shirts in the heat of New York because, compared to his home, "it was a cool snap, mon."

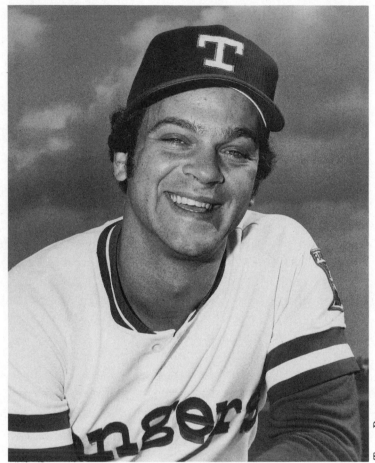

Texas Rangers

DAVID CLYDE

BORN 1955
RANGERS 1973–75
MINOR LEAGUES 1975–77
INDIANS 1978–79

*T*he telephone rang and was answered on the second ring. "McCauley Lumber," said a mature-sounding voice.

The voice belonged to David Clyde. At thirty-two, he had already been out of baseball for eight seasons. Some pitchers might now be at the top of their game. All of that is pretty far from David's mind.

In 1973, baseball was very much on his mind. He had just turned eighteen in April, and in June he was selected by the Texas Rangers as the nation's number one amateur draft choice.

At Houston's Westchester High School he had compiled a senior-year record of 18–0 with a 0.18 earned-run average. The well-built left-hander might have gone on to the minor leagues under other circumstances, but the Rangers needed him. It was their second year in Texas, and they had a lackluster ball club, drawing modestly. To elevate a home-grown Texan and throw him against big leaguers as a teenager would be a shot in the arm for the franchise.

So without any minor-league experience, David Clyde put on uniform number 34 and stood on the mound at Arlington Stadium. It was June 27, 1973, and a sellout crowd of over thirty-five thousand turned out.

Clyde walked the first two Minnesota Twins he faced, then struck out the next three. In five innings he allowed only one hit—a two-run homer—and wound up beating Jim Kaat, 4–3.

How kind history could be if only it could bottle those moments and preserve them for all time. But 1973 was before the age of home video.

David lost his next three decisions and finished the year at 4–8 with a 5.03 ERA. Determined to keep this gate attraction in the rotation, the Rangers kept him in the big leagues all of 1974, during which he was 3–9 with a 4.38 ERA. He was just not ready.

"If I had the opportunity to do things over again," he says, "there really wouldn't be a great deal I'd do differently. I was eighteen and it was a dream come true to get that kind of opportunity. I suppose some minor-league experience would have been good."

The minor-league experience finally came in 1975, when he pitched well in the Eastern League. But he never did find success in the majors. He was the object of a management feud between manager Billy Martin and the Texas

G.M., Dan O'Brien, over his role with the team. He spent all of 1976 and 1977 in the minors and had shoulder surgery to dampen his future further. In 1978 and 1979 he went to the Cleveland Indians, returning to the majors with a two-year record of 11–15. The Indians traded him back to Texas for spring training of 1980, but he was released in March and went home, finished at twenty-four. He had eighteen career victories.

Some scouts said he entered the fast lane too quickly; that his habits were poor, or rather imitative of more mature players who could handle the fast life. David married at twenty-two, but it ended in divorce.

"After my career ended, I returned to Houston," he said, "and entered my in-laws' lumber business. There comes a time when you realize you have to take care of things. I don't dwell much on the past—I'm much too busy with the business. Once in a while I'll speak at a local school, or maybe sign some autographs at work if there's been a story about me in the paper."

"I'm remarried and have two children, plus one from the first marriage, so I'm pretty busy. I go bowling now and then, or do some fishing, but those sports give me a little pain in that left shoulder. I played some slow-pitch softball for a while—played in the outfield, in fact—and man, after playing in the majors that softball looks like a basketball floating up there."

If David had spent two or three years in the minors and not come up until he was twenty-one . . . if he hadn't had the entrapped nerve in his pitching shoulder . . . if he'd taken things a little more slowly . . .

Detroit Tigers

ROCKY COLAVITO

BORN 1933
MINOR LEAGUES 1951–56
INDIANS 1955–59
TIGERS 1960–63
ATHLETICS 1964
INDIANS 1965–67
WHITE SOX 1967
DODGERS 1968
YANKEES 1968

"*I* suppose," says Rocky Colavito, "that if I hadn't been traded to the Tigers and had spent a long career in one city, things might have worked out differently. But I met some beautiful people in Detroit, not only players, so I can't really complain."

At fifty-four Colavito was reflecting back on perhaps the biggest one-for-one trade in baseball history, the deal that sent the American League batting champion, Harvey Kuenn, to Cleveland for Colavito, the league's home-run champion.

While it didn't necessarily impair Rocky's career—he hit

45 homers in 1961 for the Tigers, and 374 lifetime—it did take a player of heroic proportions out of Cleveland, a city hungry for heroes. Had he been like Ernie Banks, playing his whole career in Chicago, or Carl Yastrzemski in Boston, Stan Musial in St. Louis, or Mickey Mantle in New York, he might have "owned" the city.

"If it was up to me, I never would have left," he says of the city people seem to enjoy ridiculing. "Cleveland was great to me."

Indeed, Rocky's post baseball life has been—well, rocky. He retired after the 1968 season and for a couple of seasons was a scout and minor-league hitting instructor for the Yankees. In 1970 he got active in his father-in-law's mushroom farm in eastern Pennsylvania and worked at that, sometimes on the side, sometimes full time.

In 1972 he took a job as a television commentator for the Indians and enjoyed it, but the following season was asked to join the team's coaching staff under Ken Aspromonte.

"I'd have preferred to stay in broadcasting, because it seemed to offer more stability," he says, "but it wasn't presented to me as though I had a choice."

But coaching paid Colavito only fifteen thousand dollars a year, about the same as announcing, and he was becoming disillusioned by the pay.

"My pride was a factor," he admits. "Coaches work hard. They're the first to arrive, the last to leave. I was never afraid to work with a .150 hitter if he asked for help.

"The game was changing, too," he added. "The players' attitudes were different. They weren't as team-oriented and they seemed preoccupied with union and labor matters."

Colavito quit the Indians in 1973, then sold the mushroom business the following year. "It was a tough business," he says. "The migrant help was more difficult than you'd believe. My father-in-law wanted me to take it over, but I didn't want to."

Rocky was out of baseball until 1976, hunting, fishing, making some personal appearances. In 1976 he joined Frank Robinson's coaching staff back in Cleveland, and in Indians' style, did a lot for the money.

"I was batting instructor, first-base coach, and color man on TV. I'd work out before the games, then shower, and rush up to the booth. I only had a few minutes to prepare for the games, but I did my homework and handled it all.

"Still, it was a terrible situation. And when I couldn't get even a two-year deal from the Cleveland TV people, I was very disappointed."

The Indians made more changes, letting Colavito and Harvey Haddix go as coaches. Colavito went to work for Minute Man, Inc., a temporary help service in Cleveland, as a representative of the company. He helped open a new branch in Akron, but with the recession at its height, the office soon closed.

In 1981 Rocky built his current home in Bernville, Pennsylvania, on two acres of land, for his wife, son, daughter-in-law, and granddaughter. Then Dick Howser, who had been a teammate in Cleveland, called and asked Rocky to be a coach for him in Kansas City.

"I'd never been with a winner," he recalls. "This was a chance for a Series ring and a Series check."

But it was not to be. After coaching in 1982 and 1983, Rocky was again frustrated by the pay. Coaches were earning less than the players' minimum, and the unfairness of it all kept bothering him.

"So I left on my own again," he says. The Royals won the '84 world championship. "I'd love to get back into baseball again, but it would have to be the right deal, with some security. That coaching stuff just wasn't right."

Today Rocky makes personal appearances, stays in great shape, collects his pension, and mows his lawn. He had a great name and might have been synonymous with Cleveland had he lived out his career there, but the movement turned him into somewhat of a journeyman, albeit one who belted 374 home runs. At the time he retired that was fifteenth on the all-time list.

HARRY CRAFT

BORN 1915
MINOR LEAGUES 1935–37
REDS 1937–42
MINOR LEAGUES 1942–43,
  1946–48
MANAGER, ATHLETICS, 1957–59
MANAGER, CUBS 1961
MANAGER, COLT .45'S 1962–64

I never played baseball until I was in college," recalls Harry Craft. "In fact, football was my sport at Mississippi College. I only took up baseball so I wouldn't have to be on the track team."

From that grew a relationship with baseball that passed the half-century mark in 1985.

Craft, seventy-two, speaks with great fondness of a life of hotel rooms and expense accounts. He was a player, a coach, a manager, and a superscout, and it seems unlikely that today's high-paid players may ever deem it interesting enough to stretch baseball into a lifetime of employment.

In the major leagues, Craft broke in with Cincinnati in 1937 and was a member of their championship clubs of 1939 and 1940. But the most memorable event of those years was the suicide of catcher Willard Hershberger.

"Willard, that little rascal, was so well liked he could have run for mayor of Cincinnati," says Craft. "Such a shame. We'd come up to Boston from New York and had three doubleheaders scheduled with the Braves. We stayed at the Copley Plaza. Willard caught the first day, but Bill Mc-Kechnie [the manager] could see he was troubled. They had dinner together, and Willard told him his father had killed himself, and he was thinking of doing the same. But by the end of the meal, McKechnie felt he had lifted Willard's spirits sufficiently that the crisis had passed. After all, he couldn't put a guard in the room. And he had a roommate, Billy Baker.

"The next day, Willard didn't show up at the park. Gabe Paul, our traveling secretary, called the hotel, then went back and got an engineer to open the door. There was Willard, over the bathtub. He had borrowed a double-edge razor from Baker—Hershberger used an electric—and cut the jugular on his left side. We were told after the second game, although we suspected something was wrong. McKechnie called us to his suite and told us that it had nothing to do with the club, or any individual on the club. But I think Bill went to his grave without ever telling anyone exactly what it was."

Craft's memories then move on to his first two years as a minor-league manager, 1949 and 1950.

"I had Mickey Mantle in his first two years. His daddy drove him up from Oklahoma after high school let out and introduced him. He was shy, but he could play. Problem was, he made so many errors on easy chances at shortstop. He'd make the tough play—I can still picture it—but muff the routine ones. After the second year, I told Casey and Weiss that he was already a Triple A hitter but just a Class B shortstop. I began to work him out in the outfield before the games. It seemed inevitable that with DiMaggio nearing the end, they'd move Mantle to the outfield. And that's what happened."

Craft managed Roger Maris at Kansas City in 1959, "and after I was fired, I saw Stengel at the '59 World Series and told him the Yankees ought to try and get Maris. He raised an eyebrow and said, "I'll look into this.""

After a stop with the Cubs, where he was one of the rotating head coaches, he was the first manager of the Houston Colt .45's.

"I had Dick Farrell and Jim Owens there," he says, "and they had this reputation of being somewhat rowdy at night. I told them, 'Don't let me catch you taking our young players with you, and when I call on you, be ready.' As far as I know, they listened to me. But I knew that it was getting hard to handle this new generation of players for me. After two years of managing the Colts, I never had a desire to manage again."

Instead, Craft began a long stint as a superscout, covering major-league teams for first the Orioles, then the Yankees, and now, in semiretirement, the Giants.

"Al Rosen offered me a job to watch National League clubs when they play the Astros in Houston. It's about forty-five minutes from here in Conroe. I file reports on the players and keep up-to-date with the game. If the Astros are on the road, that's just time off for me. I stay home and catch up on my reports. That's semiretirement. It's perfect. And when the Giants won their division in 1987, I felt like I had a little hand in it. I celebrated from fifteen hundred miles away and felt great for Al."

In 1985 Harry developed a blood clot on his lungs and a problem with fluid in the brain not draining properly. He had surgery to correct both, which he weathered successfully. He lives with his wife in a home they built in 1971, where he proudly displays plaques commemorating induction into the Cincinnati Reds Hall of Fame, the Texas Professional Baseball Hall of Fame, and the Mississippi College Hall of Fame.

RAY DANDRIDGE

BORN 1913
NEGRO LEAGUES 1933–37
CARIBBEAN LEAGUES 1938–47
NEGRO LEAGUES 1948
MINOR LEAGUES 1949–53

*O*n the stage before the Baseball Library in Cooperstown, New York, Commissioner Peter Ueberroth concluded his introductory remarks for Ray Dandridge by saying, "Ladies and gentlemen, the greatest third baseman who never played in the major leagues, Ray Dandridge."

On this sentimental day in 1987 for the seventy-four-year-old gentleman, perhaps an exaggeration could be forgiven. But it struck some as odd that Ueberroth would say that, since seated among the former inductees not fifteen feet away was Judy Johnson. Johnson had been inducted twelve years earlier, cited as the "black Pie Traynor." Both were third basemen.

"It never bothered me that Judy went in," said Dandridge, "but having that nickname probably helped him a lot. In the first year they voted in Negro League players, well, of course, Satchel Paige went in. Then came Josh Gibson, and folks were calling him the black Babe Ruth. Then came Buck Leonard, a first baseman, and he was the black Lou Gehrig. So Johnson, who played the same period as Traynor, had that nickname, and it helped."

Most observers, the few that remain, attest that it was Dandridge, the little bowlegged native of Richmond, Virginia, who was the greatest third baseman of all time in the Negro League. Thus, it was a painful wait to make it to the Hall of Fame, a wait that looked unpromising as fewer and fewer black players were chosen. After the special committee disbanded, one could no longer count on even a single annual selection.

Disappointment was nothing new to Ray. There was, of course, the disappointment of not having a chance to display his considerable skills in the major leagues in his prime. But haunting him today more than that was the lost opportunity in his waning days to set foot on a major-league field, to get his name in a major-league box score.

After Jackie Robinson broke the color line by joining Montreal in 1946 and then the Dodgers in 1947, the opportunity opened up for Ray to join organized ball. He had played for sixteen years in the Negro Leagues, the Mexican League, leagues in Venezuela and Cuba. Records being sketchy, we can only assume from the word of those who saw him that he was great.

So in 1949 he signed with the Giants and was assigned to

Minneapolis of the American Association. If it was a little insulting to go to the minor leagues after so many years as a star, he took it well. He became one of the best hitters in the association and one of the most popular players in Minneapolis. But the seasons came and went, and other players passed him by. In 1950 he was voted the MVP award, but even in September, when roster sizes increased to forty, there was no call from New York.

"I'll never understand why the Giants wouldn't give me that one moment in the sun," he said. "Maybe they had an unwritten policy about no more than three Blacks on a team, and they had three. I was nearing forty, but I could still play the game." He hit .362 at age thirty-six.

His career came to a close in 1953 in the Pacific Coast League. After two seasons managing a team outside of organized baseball in Bismarck, North Dakota, Ray returned to his longtime home of Newark, New Jersey. He had saved a little money from the relatively well-paying days of the outlaw Mexican League (outlaw, that was, to white players) and lived comfortably with his wife, Florence, and three children. But unskilled and barely high-school-educated, his options were few. He wound up tending bar for the next eighteen years.

His wife died in 1961, and he remarried five years later. A few years after that he went to work for the city of Newark in their Recreation Department, working with youngsters, getting them involved in sports. He did it until 1984, when he retired and moved to Palm Bay, Florida. It was there that he got the telephone call informing him of his 1987 election to the Hall of Fame.

"Thank you," he told the sun-baked crowd in Cooperstown, "for letting me smell the roses."

California Angels

MIKE EPSTEIN

BORN 1943
MINOR LEAGUES 1965–66
ORIOLES 1966–67
SENATORS 1967–71
ATHLETICS 1971–72
RANGERS 1973
ANGELS 1973–74

*T*here have been only about 150 Jewish players in major-league history, so Mike Epstein had a unique niche for himself. As to how many Jewish cattle ranchers settled in Wyoming . . . well, Mike might have a foothold on that, too.

The legend of Mike Epstein took him from the Bronx, to suburban Westchester County, to the campus at Berkeley, and to a big signing bonus with the Orioles in 1964. Unable to dislodge Boog Powell at first base, Mike was traded to the Washington Senators, where he spent a little more than four years, before joining the Oakland A's in their glory years. At age thirty-one, in 1974, he walked away from baseball.

"I still had some offers," he says now, "even after I was out for a couple of years. The DH rule came along in 1973 and I probably could have kept playing. Sometimes I think I shortchanged myself. My wife thinks about all the money that came soon after with free agency."

A bright and sensitive bear of a man, Mike looks back and says, "You get so caught up with the daily routine— who's pitching tomorrow, when do we get to Milwaukee, things like that, that you seldom reflect on the bigger picture, the fact that you're playing major-league baseball. It's such a wonderful, phenomenal experience—it teaches you so much about life, about people, about camaraderie."

Mike had two kinds of camaraderie. One was from the Senators. "We were almost a laughingstock, we were so bad, but it made us pull together." The other was from the A's. "That's a different kind, that comes from winning. But to tell you the truth, I still have great feelings for Washington. I cut my eye teeth there. It was unfortunate that we never went on to bigger and better things there, because in 1969, Ted Williams' first year as manager, we had a great year. And it made me proud to walk down a street in Washington and have people recognize me and root for the Senators."

The Senators were fourth in the East that year, just four games out of second. Frank Howard hit forty-eight homers and Epstein added thirty. "I got the biggest thrill just sitting with Ted Williams and talking about anything," he says.

But instead of building on the success, the Senators let it get away. "I was in Michigan when I read about the Denny McLain trade," he says. We gave away half our infield and two good pitchers for McLain, who everyone knew couldn't throw anymore. The Senators' owner, Bob Short, just didn't understand talent or baseball. He liked to spend, spend, spend, but he didn't know what he was doing. In Oakland, Finley never spent, but he knew talent. We never went first class, despite our success, but we won in spite of Finley."

After the McLain fiasco, the Senators needed bodies, so Epstein and Darold Knowles were dealt to the A's for a collection of players, and Mike got into the 1972 World Series victory over Cincinnati.

Having worked winters as a cowboy in Wyoming, Mike felt that was his postbaseball calling. When he left the Angels in 1974, he moved to San Jose and worked for a precious-metals company. Sales soared over the next 2½ years, so he decided to start his own company. Four years later he had rung up sales of seventy million dollars and sold out to the largest precious-metal conglomerate in Europe, continuing as a consultant to high-tech companies.

That gave him time to go back to full-time ranching. He now has two thousand head in Wyoming and spends most of his time on horseback.

He has three children, has been married for more than twenty years, and took his nine-year-old back to RFK Stadium in Washington in 1986. "They used to paint the seats in the upper deck when Howard or I hit long homers," he says. "Frank's were white, mine were light blue. I walked up there with my son to the places those balls had gone. The paint was gone, but I couldn't believe how far from home plate it was. They were measured at over five hundred feet, but I'd never stood there looking down before."

His son, at six, had roped a steer to the amazement of onlookers, but then he discovered baseball and never picked up a rope again. "It's a great game," Mike says. "In business, you see how people, even without much personality, can come alive when the subject turns to baseball."

Mike also maintains a home in Denver so he can be in

easy commuting distance for business. He visits spring training camps, sees old friends, shares some laughs. A few years ago he called on Blue Moon Odom to help him during a personal crisis—that old baseball camaraderie coming through. Even when players have lost touch, the bond remains.

Mike retired with a .244 average and 130 home runs. Some might say the promise he held as a rookie didn't pan out, and yet he beat the odds to play major-league baseball at all. Don't think for a minute he's lost his appreciation of that.

San Francisco Giants

EDDIE FISHER

BORN 1936
MINOR LEAGUES 1958–61
GIANTS 1959–61
WHITE SOX 1962–66
ORIOLES 1966–67
INDIANS 1968
ANGELS 1969–72
WHITE SOX 1972–73
CARDINALS 1973

*W*hen Eddie Fisher broke in with the San Francisco Giants in 1959, he was not the best-known Eddie Fisher in America. But baseball, having a more lasting effect on America than pop singers do, has finally moved the right-handed knuckleballing relief star up front. It seems unlikely that the crooner who was once married to Liz Taylor gets fifty fan letters each month.

It is through the letters that Eddie is reminded of his fifteen-year career on an almost daily basis, but if the truth be told, he doesn't miss the game all that much. Whereas at one time he had trouble balancing his checkbook, today he is president of the First Federal Savings & Loan Association in Altus, Oklahoma, where he resides.

"For no particular reason, I decided to give the finance business a try when I got out of baseball in 1974. I went on to become branch manager, and today I'm president. Now I've been in the banking business almost as long as I was in baseball."

Eddie's top salary in the majors was fifty-two thousand dollars. He does better today, but "I do miss the money I would have been making if I was playing now."

Imagine if he'd been a free agent after the 1965 season, when he won fifteen, saved twenty-four, and set an American League record for games pitched, with eighty-two in one season.

The baseball from the record-setting game is part of the memorabilia in his game room, along with the ball from his first victory, recorded as a teammate of Willie Mays, Willie McCovey, and Orlando Cepeda in San Francisco.

"If I think of myself with any one team," he says, "it would be the White Sox, because I had my best years there. But I was also with the 1966 Orioles, who beat the Dodgers in the World Series for their first championship, and I have a particular fondness for the cowboy Gene Autry."

Like many former players, Fisher speaks in the most glowing terms of the legendary movie star who has owned the California Angels since they entered the major leagues. "He's a wonderful man," says Eddie, "and really just a big fan who is very close to the players. We both had similar interests, and I once traded him a rifle I owned for a pistol he'd used in a movie. That's a prized keepsake for me."

In addition to his banking responsibilities, Eddie and his son have a sporting goods store, and have had ex-Oriole teammates Boog Powell and Brooks Robinson by for store promotions. Eddie also includes Dave McNally, Joel Horlen, and John Buzhardt among close friends.

Fisher lives about three hours from Dallas, and he will see the Rangers play when business brings him to that city. With luck, he gets to see Seattle pitcher Mike Moore work. Moore was on an American Legion team Fisher coached a few years ago.

Eddie still checks the box scores daily and considers himself a good fan. One of his recent gifts from his children was the special edition coffee-table book featuring all the Topps baseball cards ever printed.

He can see himself on about fifteen pages in the book, filled with nice memories of a solid career.

At fifty-one, and twice a grandfather, Eddie enjoys the good, quiet Oklahoma life, far from the boisterous fans of Chicago.

BOB FRIEND

BORN 1930
MINOR LEAGUES 1950–51
PIRATES 1951–65
YANKEES 1966
METS 1966

---

*I*t would surprise many base-
ball fans to know that Bob Friend was thirty-three games
under .500 for his career, with a 197–230 record. He
is instead remembered as one of the better pitchers of
his time.

"Nineteen eighty-seven was the one-hundredth anniversary of the Pirates," he said, "and the club, which is very
good about alumni and history, provided stats on all of the
players. I know I lost more games than I won, but I did
pitch for many years with teams that were in developmental

stages. I was pleased to see that I still hold the Pirate records for innings pitched and strikeouts, and I think I'm fourth in career shutouts."

No one ever doubted Bob's durability, for he seldom missed a start in his sixteen seasons and twice led the league in innings pitched. But the Pirate team he joined in 1952 was a long way from the team that finally won the world championship of 1960, when Friend won eighteen games.

"Oh, 1960 was my happiest year in baseball," he says without hesitation, even though he had a 22–14 record two years earlier and had won the league's ERA title in 1955. "That '60 team has to be considered a Cinderella story, just like the 1969 Mets. It was an especially good year for almost all the guys on the team as far as individual performances go. We had a good bench and a very good pitching staff. Elroy Face had an exceptional campaign. Danny Murtaugh did a very good job managing the team, and overall it was just very exciting.

"The whole season was special. It was the first time in thirty-three years that Pittsburgh had the opportunity to play in a World Series. That final game was so exciting, and I remember the lead changing hands throughout the game. When Mazeroski finally hit the homer to win it, everybody was breathless for a moment until we realized what had happened. It really took a while to get used to it. There was bedlam throughout the city. Nowadays, you have the Steelers with four Super Bowl titles and the Pirates had all those good teams in the 1970s, so it just isn't the same."

Bob married a Pittsburgh girl in 1957. Their daughter graduated from Bob's alma mater, Purdue, and their son graduated from Louisiana State University, where he had a golf scholarship.

"As we speak, he's trying to get his pro card and hopes

to join the pro tour," said Bob, with obvious satisfaction. Bob himself is an avid golfer.

"In my home I've got a three-foot-by-four-foot blowup photo of Maz's homer, and some pictures of Forbes Field lit up at night. They're artistic in their own way."

After Bob's career ended, he got into politics, and took his degree in economics to public office, serving eight years as the Allegheny County controller. In 1975 he joined BABB, Inc., an insurance brokerage firm, where he is today vice president of sales in the marketing division.

"We have one of the luxury boxes at Three Rivers Stadium, and I get out there ten or twelve times a year, especially now with the Pirates on the upswing again. Clients like to go, and I'm pleased to see them having good time at the game. I know a couple of the team's owners through business and I've got a very keen interest in the team's revitalization."

Bob, who was the winning pitcher in two All-Star Games and who is very active in the fledgling Players' Association, applauds today's players for their economic accomplishments but sighs when he reflects on the quality of today's ball. "There aren't as many great players overall. It's the difference between playing with only sixteen teams as opposed to twenty-six."

DAVE GIUSTI

BORN 1939
MINOR LEAGUES 1961–64
COLT .45'S/ASTROS 1962–68
CARDINALS 1969
PIRATES 1970–76
CUBS 1977
ATHLETICS 1977

*I*t seemed as though Dave Giusti packed it all into his sixteen-year major-league pitching career.

He was one of the first players signed by the expansion Houston Colt .45's, and he pitched in the depths of the National League with them, mostly as a starting pitcher.

His fortunes turned around when he landed with Pittsburgh in 1970, became a relief pitcher, and worked for five championship teams, setting the league record for career saves by the time he retired.

"With Houston, of course, I was a starter, and the memories are different because there were no pennant races. But the greatest personal thrill I ever had," says Dave, "was with Houston. It was a nationally televised game on a Saturday afternoon when I faced Juan Marichal of the Giants in 1968. I pitched a one-hitter, faced only twenty-seven batters, and threw only eighty-four pitches. I'll never forget it."

On the other hand, there was the one pitch he'd love to have back.

"Oh, yes, the one that will still haunt me from time to time. It was 1972 and I was facing Johnny Bench in the bottom of the ninth inning in the final game of the playoffs. We were leading, 2–1. If we get through that inning, we're in the World Series for the second year in a row.

"But Bench hit one out to tie it up, and we lost on a wild pitch by Bob Moose later on. I heard Bench say recently that the homer was his greatest thrill in baseball.

"Those individual one-on-one duels are what I find myself missing the most," he says. "I always had problems facing two guys in particular—Billy Williams and Joe Torre. It was always interesting to try and figure out how to get certain guys out, and how you were going to do against certain teams. Funny, I had trouble with Williams, but I won more games in my career against the Cubs than any other team."

As a relief pitcher, Giusti's philosophy became very health-oriented. "Stay healthy was my credo," he says, "because you could possibly pitch in every game, whether actually getting in there, or just warming up. I was lucky to have never suffered any major injuries. My job was to get guys out and find a way to approach every hitter I faced. It was clearly a mental game."

If there is a special memory of one player, it is reserved

for Roberto Clemente. "Most people knew of his greatness," says Dave, "but it wasn't until I played with him for 162 games a year that I really appreciated his talents. He saved so many games for me in right field. They gave relief pitchers saves, but a lot of them should have been credited to Roberto. A lot of people didn't understand him. He would miss an occasional game now and then, but the truth was, he just wouldn't play the game unless he could perform at 100 percent. It was his pride."

Dave's career ended following the 1977 season. He had an offer to be a pitching coach for the Pirates, but it wasn't what he really wanted to do.

"I really wanted to open a restaurant," he says, "but I backed out when I realized the time and money involved.

"So after about a year I got a job with a company called Millcraft Products, in the engineering and steel products field. I was in sales, and I liked it.

"I did that for three years and then I joined American Express in 1982, which is where I still am, as a sales manager."

Dave, forty-eight, lives in the same home in Pittsburgh he bought in 1970, his first year with the Pirates. He and his wife have two daughters in college.

"I haven't been out of the game that long, but much of it has already changed," he notes. "It shows you how ever-changing even a traditional sport like baseball can be. Today, everything is so specialized. They even have minor leaguers training to be short relievers. When I first came up, relief pitchers were the guys not good enough to start, although very soon afterward the job became more and more important."

DICK HALL

BORN 1930
MINOR LEAGUES 1952–53,
 1955, 1957, 1959
PIRATES 1952–57, 1959
ATHLETICS 1960
ORIOLES 1961–66
PHILLIES 1967–68
ORIOLES 1969–71

*A*s big Dick Hall approaches sixty, he gets a bit more nostalgic for his days as a major-league pitcher.

"Part of it," he muses, "is that for the first time since before I was an Oriole, the team has had a bad pitching staff this year. So friends always kid me about making a comeback."

Still, with a fine pitching career behind him, it is a home run baseball he wishes he had. "It was my first major-league home run. I hit it in 1954 with the Pirates off Ernie Johnson of Milwaukee. I was an outfielder then."

Hall was signed as a bonus baby by the Pirates in 1952. The team had shelled out big dollars for the highly touted Paul Pettit, a pitcher, around that time, and Hall also came with great expectations. At six-six, generally considered too tall for a pitcher, he was ticketed to play the outfield.

Unfortunately, the bat wasn't there. In his fourth minor-league season, it was decided to try him on the mound, and he had a 12–5 record in the Western League, then joined the Bucs.

"I'd like to say that the rest was a success story," he says, "but I went back to the minors in '57 and then decided to quit."

His return to the minors in 1959 resulted in an 18–5 season and finally, a one-way ticket to the big leagues. Control would be his forte.

"There is a statistic that I am quite proud of," he says. "In my last seven years in the majors [1965–71], I only allowed twenty-three bases on balls that were not intentional walks. I also only had one wild pitch in my career, and that came when I was experimenting with a knuckleball. At Pittsburgh, Branch Rickey wanted everyone to experiment with a knuckleball."

Such great control made Hall an able reliever and a member of four championship Oriole teams. "My last three years in baseball I was in the World Series," he notes. There is irony in that, because after spending eight years with struggling Pirate teams in the 1950s, he was traded to Kansas City in December 1959. "The Pirates finally win in 1960," he says with a laugh, "and I'm sitting in Kansas City reading about it."

Hall is most closely tied to the Orioles. He speaks fondly of the Oriole teams of Frank and Brooks Robinson, Boog Powell, Jim Palmer, and Dave McNally. "These were star players," he says, "but they were team-oriented, and that made the team gel. They played as a unit."

Dick has lived outside Baltimore, in Timonium, for the past twenty-five years. He has three married daughters and five grandchildren. He was Billy Ripken's Little League coach, so his current Oriole interest is strong.

"Tim Stoddard, when he pitched here, reminded me of myself," says Hall. "Very tall, of course, and a similar role, with selected relief assignments.

"In 1972, my first year out of baseball, I had an offer to coach for Cleveland. But they trained in Arizona, and it would have meant too much time away from my family.

"In 1969 I passed my C.P.A. exam. So I was ready for a second career. But I'll tell you, I had picked up three straight World Series checks, and I found things difficult financially. The stock market wasn't doing well, and I had kids in college. But things worked out."

Hall is currently a manager in the Tax Department at the accounting firm of Peat Marwick Main & Co. He shoots golf in the eighties but he had to give up jogging after some cartilage trouble in a knee.

"I only get to five or ten Oriole games a year now," he says with a smile. "It interferes with my golf game. I've gone from a passionate viewer to more of a rooting fan."

As though to underscore Dick's value to the Orioles, the team won the 1966 world championship, lost out in 1967 and 1968, and won three pennants in a row beginning in 1969. During those two years they missed, Dick was off pitching for the Phillies. When he came back, the Orioles returned to the top. When he retired after 1971, the Orioles didn't return to the World Series for eight years.

JIM HICKMAN

BORN 1937
MINOR LEAGUES 1956–61
METS 1962–66
DODGERS 1967
CUBS 1968–73
CARDINALS 1974

"*I*f not for expansion," says Jim Hickman in that easy Tennessee drawl, "I don't know how long I would have stuck it out. It came along at the right time for me."

Hickman, remembered mostly as an original Met and a pretty good Chicago Cub, had spent six years in the Cardinals' minor-league system but saw little hope of reaching the big leagues until the Mets were born and selected him to the expansion draft.

"I really wasn't a big-leaguer yet," he says. "In fact, I

really wasn't a big-leaguer until I was thirty. But the Mets gave me a chance. The owners were great to us, and Casey Stengel, well, it was a privilege to play for him, but after a while, understandably, the fans started to turn against us. They got tired of losing. And who could blame them? We were tired of it, too."

While the original Mets were lovable, it was true that the joke was wearing thin by their fifth season. Hickman was still there, and the fans were getting on him. So it was off to the Dodgers for a year, and then on to the Cubs, where he found his stride.

"I played for Stengel, Walter Alston, and Leo Durocher in those years," he says. "That's really something to think back over. Legends."

With the Cubs he found himself on a winning team although they never did win a pennant. Still, with Banks, Santo, Williams, Beckert, and Hundley, it was a good team, and things began to fall in place for Jim.

"It's a lot easier on a good team. Guys pick each other up. It's contagious. My time just came in Chicago. I can't explain why. But I think back mostly to those Cub years. You ask me why I hit .315 one year, and I can't tell you. I thought of myself as a .270 or .280 hitter with some power, but that one year, ground balls just seemed to go through, line drives seemed to fall in, everything was right. I really can't explain how it can happen over a full season like that."

That 1970 season was a special one for Jim. He played in the All-Star Game, getting the winning hit in the twelfth inning in Cincinnati. "That was the play Pete Rose crashed into Ray Fosse to score the winning run. I'm a trivia question because I got the hit. But to tell you the truth, I was really surprised by the play. I saw it out of the corner of my eye, and I was really surprised it was so close. There were two outs. I really thought Pete would have scored easily."

To remember the event, Jim has the front page of the next morning's *Chicago Tribune* mounted on a plaque in his home. But his other baseball souvenirs are few, and his contact with former teammates slim. Until Randy Hundley began organizing Chicago Cub Fantasy Camps a few years ago, Jim was pretty much out of touch with old friends. Now he loves returning to the camps and seeing old teammates. He's still at his playing weight of 192, and at fifty, he works hard each day on his farm.

However, there is a sad story. The farm he owned for nearly two decades in Henning was lost in 1986. He had mortgaged it to pay for its operation, and the bank had to take it over. "We owe money we'll never be able to pay," he says sadly. "Things went bad. I hope someone knows the answer to what's happening to all the farms around here. I don't think anyone in Memphis does. Now I'm working on land that we lease, raising some soybeans and cotton. But it's not like having your own place."

Three of Jim's children live close by and have made him a grandfather three times over. A fourth son is at home, helping with the farming, finishing college.

"We're doing pretty well now," he says. "You start over, deal with it, and move on. We'll be all right."

More than seventeen years after his big All-Star hit in Cincinnati, the Reds telephoned. Ted Kluszewski was retiring as the team's minor-league hitting instructor. Would Jim be interested in replacing him?

"What a wonderful phone call," he said. "I'm back in uniform. It's like being a kid again."

Chicago Cubs

Glen Hobbie with
grandson Bryan Matthew

GLEN HOBBIE

BORN 1936
MINOR LEAGUES 1955–57
CUBS 1957–64
CARDINALS 1964

*L*ong-suffering Chicago Cub fans (as much of a cliché in the 1980s as it was in the 1950s) remember Glen Hobbie as one of those pitchers "who would have won twenty on any contender."

Instead, he lost twenty for the 1960 Cubs, a seventh-place team that escaped last place only because the Phillies were even worse in those days.

But that twenty-loss season, according to Hobbie, "was my best, my most memorable year." A closer look at the record shows that Hobbie was the only Cub hurler to win more than nine that season, and his sixteen victories were all complete games, a remarkable accomplishment by today's standards.

Oddly, a look at the Cub roster that lost 94 that season shows some pretty fair names. Ernie Banks, still at shortstop, hit forty-one homers to lead the league. Ron Santo, Richie Ashburn, George Altman, and Frank Thomas were in the lineup. It was pre-expansion, and baseball talent might have been at its peak.

"Today's players are excellent," says Hobbie, now fifty-one. "But it's hard to really evaluate just how good they are. There are so many stadiums with artificial surfaces; you have balls skipping through the infield and bloop hits taking crazy bounces over outfielders' heads."

Like many ex-Cubs, Hobbie's heart is still in the friendly confines of Wrigley Field, natural grass and all. "It was a great place to play," he says. "The fans always seemed to be a part of the game, being as close to the field as they were. It was a good old place to play baseball."

In a way, it helped curb a tendency Hobbie had to take his responsibilities somewhat loosely. "It was better for family life to play in Chicago," he explains. "It gave a player an opportunity to have, in essence, a nine-to-five job instead of getting home at two in the morning and sleeping until ten. By the time you wake up, the kids are off in school already."

Hobbie, who married in 1959, did have his best years in 1959 and 1960, winning thirty-two of his lifetime sixty-two victories. "If I could start all over again," he adds, "I would definitely have been more serious in my approach to the game. I was only twenty-two when I came up . . . awfully young at the time. There was probably room for better effort."

Even three decades later, Hobbie can be an inspiration to struggling minor-league players. He was signed in 1955, and his first two minor-league seasons were plagued by a nagging back injury; he felt he was on the verge of getting released. Assigned to Memphis in 1957, the back pain suddenly cleared up, and he won fifteen games, earning a promotion to the majors at the end of the season. "It was," he says, "my happiest year in pro ball."

It ended for Hobbie with the pennant-winning Cardinals in 1964. He was traded for Lew Burdette but pitched only thirteen times and didn't stick around long enough to be eligible for the World Series.

"For a Cubbie to make it to a World Series would have been a treat," he says. "I didn't get there, but Lou Brock did. Same year."

With his eight-year career over, Hobbie went to work for the Roller Derby Skate Company, near his home in Hillsboro, Illinois. He's still there, serving as plant supervisor.

Only eleven hundred people live here," he says, "so everyone knows of my background. I still get letters from collectors, and I still follow the Cubs closely, although I don't go to games, because I dislike crowds. That's why I like Hillsboro, I guess."

Hobbie keeps in touch with a few contemporaries, including Dick Schofield, whose son now plays shortstop for the Angels. "Dick was everyone's former teammate," he says, recalling that the senior Schofield played nineteen years for seven teams, "but we never played together. Still, he was a friend. He got me an autographed baseball from the 1960 champion Pirates which I still have."

MONTE IRVIN

**BORN 1919
NEGRO LEAGUES 1938–48
GIANTS 1949–55
CUBS 1956**

---

*A*nyone who knows Monte Irvin would categorize him as a soft-spoken gentleman of warmth and modesty. But within him is a great deal of well-deserved pride, which can slip out on occasion. Such an example was in a recent conversation with a friend.

"Monte," he was asked, "when you broke into the Negro Leagues, which player were you most like in today's market? George Foster? Dave Parker? Jim Rice?"

"Oh, DiMaggio," he replied without hesitation. He smiled as he realized it didn't sound very modest. But the comparison was obviously well-established in his mind.

Indeed, many would confirm that the greatest schoolboy athlete in New Jersey history might well have been that good.

But timing is everything in life. Monte missed playing in the majors during his peak years because of the color line. He could have achieved Jackie Robinson's fame but was passed over as the first black player. He would have won the MVP award for the 1951 World Series—a .458 average, a steal of home, brilliant defense—but they didn't give that award then. And, of course, he missed out on the big money and had to continue working after his playing days, even at age sixty-eight, serving, as this is written, as a vice president for a Long Island investment firm. Before that he spent many years as a special assistant to Commissioner Bowie Kuhn, and before that, represented a Brooklyn brewery. He's always taken good care of his family, but compared to today's stars, one feels he ought not to have been commuting to a job into his sixties.

He says there is no question he could have accomplished what Jackie Robinson did, but would have gone about it with a smile.

"I would have handled it. I like people. I would have told the Cardinals, 'Hey, you guys are supposed to be classier than this.' "

Monte had a cool and distant relationship with Robinson, partly due to the rivalry between the Dodgers and Giants. But when he worked for Rheingold Breweries, he got Jackie a huge endorsement contract.

"Jackie said he wouldn't endorse a beer," says Monte. "But when the price got right, he agreed to admit that he was happy to serve it in his home."

Monte was a close friend of the late Josh Gibson, the acknowledged best hitter of the Negro Leagues. "Oh, was he strong," says Irvin. "I wish somehow I could find films of him hitting. What an instructional film it would be. And Josh was the sort who would never get mad. Never saw him get mad in all the years I knew him. He was the greatest kidder in the world. But in his last year, when he knew he wasn't going to get better, he said to me, 'Monte, you don't know how much I admire you.' And I said, 'You admire me? It's me who admires you!' "

Under Leo Durocher, Monte served the role of big brother to a rookie named Willie Mays, happy to give advice. Is he still the "big brother" today? "Willie gives me advice today," he says. "I just listen."

After he retired from the commissioner's office in 1984, Monte and his wife, Dee, moved to Homosassa, Florida, the longtime home of Dazzy Vance. But Monte still travels a great deal and has friends to look up at every stop, including grandchildren in Houston, and people like Al Lopez, Roy Campanella, Ernie Banks, Gabe Paul, and others from his long involvement in the game.

While he turned over most of his memorabilia to the Baseball Hall of Fame, into which he was inducted in 1973, he still has his 1936 New Jersey State javelin throwing trophy, for a toss of 192 feet, 2 inches. He was all-state in four sports for three consecutive years in high school, and there are two baseball parks named for him in the state.

In 1949 Mrs. Effa Manley, owner of the Newark Eagles of the Negro National League, sold Monte's contract to Horace Stoneham of the Giants for five thousand dollars. Branch Rickey of the Dodgers never paid the Negro Leagues for players, so Stoneham's gesture was generous under the circumstances. Monte decided to ask Mrs. Manley for half the purchase price.

"She turned me down, and went out and bought herself a

fur stole," he recalls. "Then in 1982, shortly before she died, there was a gathering in Ashland, Kentucky, for alumni of the Negro Leagues, and she was being honored. It was the middle of the summer, but she showed up wearing that stole. I went over to her—she was about eighty—and said, 'Mrs. Manley, isn't that me you're wearing over your shoulders?' She laughed and said, 'Oh, Monte, you never forget.' "

Because of all his time in Bowie Kuhn's office, Monte is as up-to-date on modern baseball as he is recalling events of forty years ago in Mexico, Cuba, or Puerto Rico, where he remains legendary. One statistical quirk that preys on his mind is his ninty-nine career home runs in the majors.

"I probably hit about four-hundred in the Negro Leagues," he says, "but I wish I had one more in the majors. Every now and then someone publishes a list of most home runs by players alphabetically—you know: A Aaron 755, B Banks 512, C Cepeda 379, and so on. My ninety-nine kind of sticks out like a sore thumb when you get to 'I.' But I have a letter from a Dodger fan, sent to Commissioner Ueberroth just a couple of months ago, who finally confesses that one I hit in Ebbets Field in 1956 that was ruled a double was actually a home run. He caught it. But he hated the Giants so much he couldn't admit it until now, even though I was with the Cubs then. I wish I could get that hundredth homer," he says with a chuckle.

"Anyway, it's kind of academic. Pete Incaviglia will pass me in a year or two."

CLEM LABINE

BORN 1926
MINOR LEAGUES 1944,
  1946–52
DODGERS 1950–60
TIGERS 1960
PIRATES 1960–61
METS 1962

Clem Labine was a master relief pitcher for the legendary "Boys of Summer" who played their hearts out in Ebbets Field, borough of Brooklyn, New York.

"There were, of course, no 'Boys of Summer' back then," he notes, speaking from his new villa in Woonsocket, Rhode Island. "We were just the Brooklyn Dodgers, a very good team, a World Championship team, but we had no nickname, except for 'Bums.'

"Then Roger Kahn wrote his book *The Boys of Summer*

and made us all nationally known figures, not just Brooklyn favorites. There were no 'Boys of Summer' until the 1970s. Thank you, Roger. You made us special."

Indeed, Kahn's book did create a mystique, and a following that might just have been slipping away. It also made the players speak their deep feelings about life in Brooklyn, which Labine still proclaims today.

"What they lost in Brooklyn can never be replaced," he says. "They lost their soul, they lost their self-esteem. It wasn't just the ball club. It was the generational thing, grandfathers passing on Dodger stories to their grandchildren, generations rooting for this neighborhood team. When I lived in Bay Ridge, a section of Brooklyn, it was just the friendliest place I ever lived in in my life. You were never lacking for a baby-sitter, never lacking for pasta. We all lived in Brooklyn, and we all loved it. There were thirty thousand people there two years ago for a reunion when they set up a Dodger Hall of Fame, and it was just so wonderful to see, even to see kids who never knew a Brooklyn Dodger team."

Although he calls the move to Los Angeles "very difficult," he still says the Dodgers are a first-class organization and has a world of respect for Peter O'Malley, the current president. "Did you know he flew us all down to Vero Beach for a thirtieth reunion of the 1955 champions? I'm very proud to have been a member of that organization."

Labine broke in with the Dodgers in 1950 and was part of six championship Dodger teams on two coasts. He has a plaque designating him as Fireman of the Year for 1956 "before they actually had such an award," he says. He has his rings and his Brooklyn uniforms—"the first things collectors want to buy from you."

Labine's four children are all married, and a stepdaughter is in law school. With the children out of the house, Clem and his second wife, Barbara (his first passed away), moved into their villa in 1985. Most of his memorabilia was stored away then, "although Barbara selected some photos for a collage we have hanging up."

He also changed careers. For many years he worked in the apparel business, catering to customers purchasing sportswear. "Three years ago, a friend, the chief executive officer of the Eastland Bank here, said he had a place for me. And at fifty-nine I became a banker. I am a business development officer. It's very interesting. You could say I took a page out of Carl Erskine's book—he's a banker, too."

Clem's son Jay, written about in *The Boys of Summer*, had lost a leg in Vietnam. "He's found himself," says Clem. "He's adjusted. He works for the Department of Transportation here in Rhode Island."

Clem pitched for the Tigers, Pirates, and Mets after his Dodger career ended in 1960, getting one last World Series in with the '60 Bucs.

"I only pitched fourteen games for the Tigers before I went back to the National League," he recalls. "The Dodgers were good to send me there, because they had a terrific team. But it was hard to give up my teammates, and the American League seemed so different. I went to a club that was in contention, but they seemed to lack a team spirit. They probably didn't, you understand, but I was coming over from something very, very special."

TED LEPCIO

BORN 1930
MINOR LEAGUES 1951–52
RED SOX 1952–59
TIGERS 1959
PHILLIES 1960
WHITE SOX 1961
TWINS 1961

*T*ed Lepcio was a utility infielder with the Boston Red Sox during the 1950s, a time, he says, very different from today.

"For one thing," he notes, "you really didn't complain if the manager sat you down. We all felt so thankful just to be in the big leagues. For a player like myself, it was a dream; you just didn't complain about all the maneuvering. But, of course, you'd sit for five or six games, and then go out and hit against Herb Score or Billy Pierce or Whitey Ford, and then they'd sit you down again. It was tough.

"There was a time, early on, when I thought I could break through and play more regularly. I looked forward to playing next to Johnny Pesky and learning from him. But the Red Sox in those days tended to move a lot of guys in and out, and it was hard to establish stability. At one point they even tried Jimmy Piersall at short, and that was a disaster."

With a smile at the recall of Piersall, Lepcio spoke about the 1957 movie *Fear Strikes Out,* which starred Anthony Perkins as the troubled Piersall seeking to overcome mental illness.

"Oh, that movie was a farce," he says. "They wanted to use real players, and they came to us to get us to cooperate on a volunteer basis. Imagine that. We weren't as sophisticated as today's players when it came to endorsements and all, but even then we knew that was ridiculous. So no players participated, and I think it showed. They didn't do a very good job with that movie."

Lepcio, who played second, shortstop, and third base in three different Opening Day lineups for the Red Sox, does have fond words for his relationship and his memories of the great Ted Williams, the Sox' dominant star of the period.

"We had a wonderful relationship," he says. "He was really inspirational. He told me I should have done better; he was a perfectionist, maybe a little eccentric, but he was a genius in his field, and I guess all geniuses can be a little eccentric."

Of Tom Yawkey, the Red Sox owner, Ted has these thoughts: "I think he was a different man after that 1967 pennant, when he was very much a part of the scene. In the fifties he was much more introverted, not outgoing at all. In our days, he'd pretty much disappear when the club-house filled with players. He'd talk to Ted, or Billy Goodman or Mel Parnell, but none of us really had a one-on-one with him, like you'd hear later on. But the organization was always first class."

Ted is still close to the organization today, having lived in the Boston area since his rookie season of 1952. Although a Utica, New York, native, his New England accent is pronounced. He is active with the Bosox Club, succeeding Dominick DiMaggio to become its second president, and he helps arrange ten luncheons each year with Red Sox and visiting personnel.

"It certainly keeps me close to the game," he says. "I can still see old friends like Sparky Anderson, Billy Consolo, you name them, when teams come to town. We were all very close back in the fifties. Remember, there were only eight teams, and you'd play each opponent twenty-two times. You'd really develop friendships, even with other teams. When Al Kaline went into the Hall of Fame, he sent us a memento. When Harmon Killebrew went in, I drove to Cooperstown for it. We were all close back then."

He sees former teammates like Frank Malzone, Ike Delock, and Dick Gernert regularly, and still savors every moment of his baseball days.

His home in Dedham is shared with his wife and sixteen-year-old son, whom Ted fathered at forty-one.

When he retired after disc surgery in 1961, "I wasn't one to ask for a job in baseball," so he went to work heading up a sales training team for Honeywell, and for the past fifteen years has done work in an executive capacity with St. Johnsbury Trucking, the largest regional carrier in the United States. He currently serves as director of national accounts.

"I'd have liked to have been a regular," says Ted, who topped a hundred games only once, "but a least I had the talent to put in ten years at a time when the minor leagues were loaded with guys anxious to take your job. It was a great time to be a ballplayer."

SPARKY LYLE

BORN 1944
MINOR LEAGUES 1964–67
RED SOX 1967–71
YANKEES 1972–78
RANGERS 1979–80
PHILLIES 1980–82
WHITE SOX 1982

*I*n an industry that was basically fun and games, few people ever took the meaning so literally as did Sparky Lyle. It is doubtful that anyone ever enjoyed baseball more, and just as likely that Sparky would have enjoyed his life no matter what occupation he had landed in.

"I had fun every day," he says from his home in southern New Jersey. "I loved going out to the park early. It was a great life."

Lyle was the purest relief pitcher of all time. He made

899 major-league appearances without ever getting a start, a record. "I never had a desire to start," he says. "Not even once."

Indeed, Lyle helped change baseball. While not the first of the modern relievers, he may well have been the first to end managers' perception of the need to have a righty-lefty tandem available in the bullpen. Lyle proved that one effective and dominating relief ace could work to both left-handers and right-handers. Today all successful relief stars have equal success against all hitters.

"I wish I was still playing," he notes, "but I knew when it was over. I'd look at the on-deck circle and see two rookies fighting over who was going to get to hit against me."

Lyle pitched for the Red Sox, the Yankees, the Rangers, the Phillies, and the White Sox between 1967 and 1982, but it was his Yankee years that give him his greatest memories. And although his best-selling book *The Bronx Zoo* created a lot of controversy around Yankee Stadium, he has never regretted it. "I'm glad I wrote it," he says with a chuckle. "I hear more about it now than before. People always ask where they can get a copy. I was very happy with it."

He still follows the game but avoids visiting clubhouses. "I remember when I was playing and old timers would come by . . . they'd never know what to say, and you wouldn't know what to say to them. It's awkward. I wouldn't want any of that."

He gets a lot of fan mail, and "I let it pile up so it looks like a lot more." But he eventually gets around to answering it with his wife, Mary, and son Scott, now a Little Leaguer. (He has two older sons from a first marriage.) "Scott plays Little League now. Were we that bad at age seven?" he asks.

For keepsakes, as you might expect, Sparky has some

unique items. "I have my glove bronzed from my first season with the Yankees, 1972, when I had thirty-five saves. I have the actual pitching rubber from the old Yankee Stadium, which I got after the 1973 season. Nobody really knows what it is, because few people have ever seen a pitching rubber out of the ground. It's about six inches thick, and I've got it in a pot with a fern growing out of it."

He also has some old uniforms ("Not that I can fit in any of them anymore"), and a base from Busch Stadium in St. Louis.

"In my last ten years, because of the DH and pitching short relief, I only had eight at-bats. One day with the Phillies, I borrowed a bat from Pete Rose and got a base hit. There I was on first, with a helmet and a jacket, feeling pretty strange, and Rose is telling the umpire that he's gonna try *my* bat. Well, we hit and run, and don't you know, I wind up on second with a stolen base. After the game I received the base from two guys on the Cards, autographed, 'To Sparky Lyle—Your first #$%$# stolen base and probably your last. Bruce Sutter and Jim Kaat, 9/23/81.' "

Lyle keeps active today doing charity and promotional work for Atlantic City's Claridge Hotel. The job involves representing the hotel at golf tournaments or telethons or dinners, and greeting guests within the hotel itself. With so much of Atlantic City's business from the New York area, Sparky is at once recognized and one of the most popular figures on the Boardwalk.

"When Commissioner Kuhn barred Willie Mays and Mickey Mantle from baseball as long as they worked at the casino, I was a little insulted that he didn't mention me," says Sparky with a laugh. "I mean, I may not be in their class, but hey . . .

"Then Commissioner Ueberroth lifts the ban, and he's on

the cover of *Sports Illustrated* with Willie and Mickey. What about ol' Sparky? Chopped liver?"

Sparky has also done some cable television work and would like to break into broadcasting. He's part of the Miller Lite advertising campaign, and with his big mustache, one the most recognizable players around.

With the gift of the strong left arm and the gift of laughter, he was a baseball star. Without the arm, he might have been a Pennsylvania truck driver, but he would have loved it and been the first guy in the garage every morning.

Denny McLain

DENNY McLAIN

BORN 1944
MINOR LEAGUES 1962–64
TIGERS 1963–70
SENATORS 1971
ATHLETICS 1972
BRAVES 1972
MINOR LEAGUES 1973

*T*o know the rocky road Denny McLain has traveled, it is almost hard to remember that when he was at the top of his game, there was no one with a smoother delivery.

He had such an effortless motion, it appeared he would pitch forever. There was nothing in indicate that a sore arm might be in his future. Or worse.

He got out of prison in August 1987 after having served twenty-nine months at Talladega, Alabama, where he had been serving an eight-year sentence for racketeering and extortion and fifteen years for cocaine possession.

"I said at the time I was sentenced that I wasn't a bum, a crook, or a dope peddler," he said. A federal appeals court had thrown out the sentence, claiming that McLain was denied a fair trail because of reversible errors made by the U.S. District Court judge and federal prosecutors. The possibility still existed that he could one day return to prison if a new trial was held. He is trying not to think about it.

When the two-time Cy Young Award winner was "sprung," he immediately contacted his old network of supporters and friends to begin piecing his life back together. His wife of twenty-four years, the former Sharon Boudreau, daughter of Hall of Famer Lou Boudreau, was living in a town house in Tampa, Florida, with the rent paid by the baseball alumni organization BAT, which helps players in need. McLain had been forced to sell his home and even his most cherished baseball mementos—his Cy Young plaques and his 1968 MVP plaque.

Then his old network came to the rescue. David Welker, an old buddy in Fort Wayne, Indiana, put him to work as a good will ambassador for the Fort Wayne Komets of the International Hockey League. Welker, who also owns a wine cooler distributorship, employed Denny there, too. He had an income.

He began making appearances at card collectors' shows. A one-inch ad in *Sports Collectors Digest* told readers that by calling Walter's Deli in Bayonne, New Jersey, arrangements could be made to have McLain appear at a show.

"He gets seventeen hundred dollars for three hours of autographing, plus expenses," they inform a caller at the deli. "He'll definitely show up, but book early. He's very much in demand." He was quickly booked for twenty appearances.

McLain was the major leagues' last thirty-game winner, chalking up thirty-one victories in 1968, the year the Tigers won the world championship. Nineteen years later, as he emerged from prison, the idea of winning thirty in the majors seemed remote.

With 24 victories in 1969, sharing the Cy Young Award with Baltimore's Mike Cuellar, Denny had 114 victories before his twenty-sixth birthday. No one thought there were only seventeen wins left in that right arm.

In 1970 he was suspended three times: for his connection with a bookmaking operation, for carrying a pistol on a flight, and for dousing two sportswriters with buckets of water. Some thought it was just ol' fun-loving Denny. He was 3–5 in 1970 and out of the majors by 1973.

Out of baseball, he ballooned from 186 pounds to over 300, and he had a heart attack in 1981. He now weighs about 140.

He tried a number of legitimate occupations, including work as a night club entertainer (he was a reasonably accomplished organist) and operating a minor-league club (Memphis).

He filed for bankruptcy in 1977. Two years later, his Lakeland, Florida, home burned down. He moved to Tampa and became office manager for a mortgage company. When it folded, he got involved with emergency walk-in clinics in Plant City and Bradenton, the latter soon shutting down.

"I was guilty of a lot of things," he said, "bad judgment, bad investments, being a little rowdy, maybe. I was no angel, but I wasn't guilty of any of the charges."

The release from prison did little to convince McLain followers that he was indeed "clean," but the legal system had hung a curve in Denny's direction, and he was back in circulation. Even his friends wondered what his next bit of mischief might be, or if things might straighten out for Denny. As he prepared to move his family out of Tampa and get on with his still young life, the trimmer and still confident McLain quite clearly had a lot of ground to make up.

In November 1987, the U.S. attorney's office in Tampa announced that McLain would be retried in 1988.

Texas Rangers

GEORGE MEDICH

BORN 1948
MINOR LEAGUES 1970–72
YANKEES 1972–75
PIRATES 1976
ATHLETICS 1977
MARINERS 1977
METS 1977
RANGERS 1978–82
BREWERS 1982

When you think of what George Medich went through to get where he is today, and how close he came to losing it, you can only be relieved, with him, that his triumphs outmaneuvered his tragedies.

Throughout his professional career, he worked hard at being a good pitcher, and hard at completing his medical studies. While other players enjoyed the fun of road trips, Medich carried *Gray's Anatomy* and studied in his room. While other players went fishing in the off-season, George went back to the University of Pittsburgh and continued the long struggle to earn his medical degree.

He got it. The seemingly impossible task of balancing two careers worked. He won 124 games in the majors. His final appearance in uniform was in a World Series. And he could scrawl "M.D." after his name if he chose to while autographing a baseball.

Then perhaps the pressures caught up with him. He speaks with caution about it. It happened in his first year out of baseball, 1983.

"After my career ended," he says, "I had to overcome a personal problem. I had a chemical dependency. I'll only say that the situation was resolved satisfactorily. There were no punitive measures taken."

George's desire to mention his problem in a few sentences hardly dramatizes what a disaster he courted. Baseball fans read all too often of wealthy players indulging themselves on cocaine for a few laughs. That is in itself an ugly enough blemish for baseball. But here was one of the game's finest examples showing that a drug problem need not be "recreational," need not involve illegal substances, and can hit anyone, even one medically astute to the dangers of prescription drugs.

The pressures of balancing the two careers quite obviously placed a great strain on Medich. For years he had not a day off to ease his mind from the texts of the medical books to the strengths of American League hitters. The baseball season would end and George would be at the hospital the next morning. Everyone thought he was amazing; no one thought the mature, well-educated Medich might be fighting demons off.

Another old Yankee, Bobby Brown, pursued a medical career while playing ball. Medich communicated with him often in his early days as a baseball player.

"He advised me against it at first," says George, "but eventually he came around and was supportive."

Perhaps Brown, now the American League president, did indeed know something of the pressures.

As one might expect, George is far too involved in his medical practice now to be much of a fan. He specializes in orthopedic surgery in Aliquippa, Pennsylvania, his birth-place. His field is appropriate for one so closely tied to sports. He lives on twenty-six acres of land in Beaver County, about twenty miles outside of Pittsburgh.

He follows the Pirates, for whom he played in 1976, and is a member of the Pirates' Almuni Association. He spent five seasons with the Texas Rangers and most closely associates his career with that organization. But it is 1973 that he remembers most fondly.

"When I came up [with the New York Yankees], there wasn't a great deal of pressure on me to begin with. I kind of snuck up on people with my performance."

He did indeed. He was 14–9 as a rookie, with only forty-one minor-league games behind him. The following year he reached a career-high nineteen victories and almost pitched the Yankees to a pennant.

"When I see Jack Morris pitch," he says, "I think of my career. Similar style. I began as a power pitcher and changed later when my fastball left.

"Baseball is not on my mind every day anymore. I don't really miss it a lot, but I will think about it occasionally when I hear a few scores."

"Doc," now thirty-nine, and his wife, Donna, have a four-teen-year-old daughter and a ten-year-old son. His children tend to think of him more as a doctor, but this is not so with neighbors or patients.

"Kids in the area are sort of too young to know me as a player, but their parents do. Once in a while someone comes by the house for an autograph. But if I'm ever asked to lecture now, the topic is usually sports medicine."

Medich's field has been one of great advancement, even from his own playing days. It's one medical field where keeping posted on new advances is essential.

"I think my years in baseball help me to better understand the kinds of problems I see each day now," he says. "Arthroscopic surgery has extended the careers of so many athletes who otherwise would have been through. Recovery time has been cut in half in many cases."

Is the Medich story a success story? It came close to crashing, but it's back on course.

Atlanta Braves

JIM PENDLETON

BORN 1924
NEGRO LEAGUES 1948–49
MINOR LEAGUES 1949–52
BRAVES 1953–56
MINOR LEAGUES 1955–56
PIRATES 1957–58
MINOR LEAGUES 1958
REDS 1959
MINOR LEAGUES 1960–61
COLT .45'S 1962
MINOR LEAGUES 1963

*T*om Seaver, in describing his childhood, spoke of rooting for the Milwaukee Braves.

"I loved their uniforms, and I loved their hitters . . . Aaron, Mathews, Adcock, even Jim Pendleton," he said.

Jim Pendleton?

When this was reported to sixty-three-year-old Jim Pendleton at his home in Houston, Texas, he laughed and said he'd never heard that before. "But that's very fine," he said. "He's a fine young man, Seaver."

The polite, soft-spoken Pendleton, though residing in a

major-league city, is far from his days as a journeyman outfielder who was part of the first Milwaukee Braves team
(1953) and the first Houston Colt .45's team, nine years
later. He was back at the twentieth reunion of the Colt .45's
in 1982, but it was his last baseball outing, save for an occasional visit to the Astrodome, where he sits, anony-
mously, as just another fan.

"The parks today—they're so big, it's sort of a hassle,
with the elevators and all. I wouldn't mind introducing myself to Terry Pendleton [no relation] of the Cardinals someday, but it's not easy to get around."

Pendleton began in the Negro Leagues in 1948 and 1949,
first with Asheville, then with the Chicago American Giants.
He played winter ball in Venezuela, where he was discovered by the Dodger scout Fresco Thompson. A shortstop,
Pendleton teamed with Jim Gilliam to form a dandy double-
play combination at St. Paul in the early 1950s, but the
Dodgers had Pee Wee Reese at short, and Jim was traded
to the Boston Braves just before spring training of 1953.

"We were in training camp, and we didn't know if we
were going to Boston or Milwaukee for the start of the season," he recalls. "We were all hoping it would be Milwaukee, because Boston was really a Red Sox town."

It was Milwaukee, and Jim hit .299 in 120 games for the
original Milwaukee Braves, who also had another kid named
Henry Aaron, ready to come up the following year. Over
the next few years, Pendleton did his time up and down,
playing regularly, riding the bench, going to the minors, traded
to Pittsburgh, traded to Cincinnati, back to the minors, up
with Houston, and finally back to the minors in '63 to wrap
it up. He was a journeyman's journeyman. His top salary
was thirteen thousand dollars.

"I liked Houston, that first year, and my second wife was

from San Antonio, so we thought we'd settle in Texas," he
explains. Right after his pro career ended, he played in a
fast-pitch semipro league in Wichita (with Bob Boyd) and
drove a bus during the season until 1966. Then he bought
his home in Houston and drove a furniture delivery truck
for many years.

Now he is security guard at Weiner's Department Store.
"Nobody knew I used to play ball, but then word got and
now some of my fellow workers talk to me about it. And
sometimes I get a baseball card sent to me in the mail to
autograph."

His 3:30 to 9:00 P.M. shift at Weiner's keeps him from
going to more games at the Dome, but he'll catch some
night games of the Braves on cable TV. He never had an
offer to work in baseball, although he did make one attempt
when Grady Hatton was working for the Astros.

"I've lost touch with my teammates," Pendleton says, "but
I think a few of them live around here—[Hal] Woodeshick,
and maybe [Hal] Smith. I'm not sure."

Pendleton remembers playing for the Havana Sugar Kings
of the International League in 1960, the year they were
transferred to Jersey City and pro baseball ended its involvement in Cuba. "Castro didn't give us any trouble—in
fact, he was quite a fan and came to a number of the games,"
Jim recalls. "But the league thought it was best for us to
move out."

At a promotion night at the Astrodome not long ago, the
Astros gave out books to all attending fans with pictures of
all the Houston baseball cards since 1962. Figuring he was
in there, Jim had his wife call the Astros.

"They sent me a book." he said. "I really appreciated it.
It's the only souvenir of my playing days I have."

Boston Red Sox

GARY PETERS

BORN 1937
MINOR LEAGUES 1956–62
WHITE SOX 1959–69
RED SOX 1970–72

*I*t seemed like it took forever for Gary Peters to become a major-league star, especially considering the talent that was waiting to emerge.

"I was a late bloomer," he says with a smile, "but you see, my high school didn't have a baseball team. Basketball was my sport. The little baseball I got in was of the sandlot variety. And I was a first baseman in those days. It was as a first baseman that the White Sox first scouted me."

So the progress was slow. Not until he was twenty-six did Gary put in a full season in the majors. But what a season it was—a 19–8 record with four shutouts and a league-leading 2.33 earned-run average. He won the Rookie of the Year award.

He was able to follow that up with an All-Star season of 20–8 in 1964.

"Oh, that would have to be my most exciting season," he recalls. "We were in a hot pennant race and wound up losing by just one game."

So Gary was 39–16 in his first two full seasons, and although he never quite reached those levels again, he was a capable and durable starting pitcher into his mid-thirties and wound up winning 124 games.

"Oh, I won a hundred or so," was the best he could recall when asked about his statistics. One might have expected a better head for figures from this math major who studied at Grove City College in Pennsylvania.

Gary's road to the majors included brief visits to the White Sox in four consecutive seasons, beginning with their pennant-winning campaign of 1959. In the four seasons he made twelve relief appearances but didn't win a game.

"I spent fourteen seasons in the White Sox organization," says Gary, "so of course I feel pretty close to them even today. That's a long association with one franchise, particularly one that doesn't win pennants and changes personnel a lot. In fact, when my career ended, the White Sox offered me a job as a pitching coach, but to be honest with you, I just wasn't interested."

Putting his math and engineering training to work, Gary accepted a job with a construction company.

"Here in Sarasota, where the White Sox train, I'm general superintendent for E. E. Simmons, still involved in construction. Each year when the teams come South, I go over to Payne Park, but to tell you the truth, there really aren't many people left in the organization that I know. Once the ownership changes, the front office people, the scouts, the minor-league managers, all seem to change, too."

Gary retired the year before the designated hitter rule came in, a rule he would have disliked. He was a good-hitting pitcher, with nineteen career homers, and with a .271 average for Boston in 1971. He was often used as a pinch-hitter and was by no means an automatic out. It dated, no doubt, to his sandlot training as a first baseman.

"Kids will stop by on occasion to show me baseball cards or get an autograph," he says, "but their heroes are today's players, and that's the way it should be. If baseball wasn't turning out new heroes, it would be in a lot of trouble."

Gary has two married daughters, one in Chattanooga, one in Atlanta. He's still in fine shape at fifty, and still enjoys the times he can put on his old White Sox uniform for a reunion game or a fantasy camp experience.

"My baseball years were great—I can't believe how many seasons have passed since I retired," he says. "You've got Toronto and Seattle, two teams I never faced, already more than a decade old. The years go quickly."

BOB PURKEY

BORN 1929
MINOR LEAGUES 1948–50,
 1953
PIRATES 1954–57
MINOR LEAGUES 1955–56
REDS 1958–64
CARDINALS 1965
PIRATES 1966

*I*t was, in a sense, the art of pitching that carried Bob Purkey through the triumph and tragedy of his postbaseball life.

"The self-discipline of pitching helped me come to terms with things, helped me analyze things, kept me going," he said.

"When you're a pitcher, you are always doing analysis. You study the hitters. You remember what they hit, what they don't. You file it all away, and you approach each hitter with the knowledge you've stored. It gives you a sense of discipline, a sense of order."

It helped Bob in the insurance business he began as his career was winding down in the mid-1960s.

"I began experiencing shoulder problems toward the end of my days in Cincinnati," he says. "I could see that I wouldn't have that many seasons left. So I began to learn the insurance business; took care of my licensing. The day after I retired, I was at a desk in my new life. And I've been running this business now for twenty-one years, longer than I was an athlete."

His independent insurance agency is in Bethel Park, Pennsylvania, three minutes from his home and not far from the site of old Forbes Field, where he made his major-league debut in 1954.

If you've ever seen photos of the Pirates in those days, you've noticed that they wore helmets rather than caps in the field. It remains a baseball oddity.

"Branch Rickey, who I think also had an interest in the helmet company, had batters wear them," Purkey recalls. "Then he had base runners wear them, and eventually we wore them in the field. I suppose it seems strange to think of pitchers wearing helmets, but it didn't bother me. It was comfortable enough. I got used to it.

"One day a throw by Roy Smalley hit our pitcher Paul Pettit in the front of his head. It split the helmet. But Paul just got up and walked off the field. After that, no one complained much about wearing them."

But back to the self-discipline.

"We lost our eighteen-year-old son Bob, Jr., in 1974," says Bob, now fifty-eight. "He was a ballplayer at Gulf Coast Junior College, and he'd been drafted by the Dodgers. He was at Grand Junction, Colorado, in a junior college swimming tournament. He won his race, then collapsed in the pool and died of cardiac arrest. It was discovered that he had a problematic blood vessel.

"I don't mind your bringing it up," he continued. "I think about it every day anyway. But again, I think that the self-discipline of pitching took me through it, enabled me to deal with it."

Just seven pounds over his playing weight and a weekly golfer, Bob lives a comfortable life, sharing his home with his wife and his in-laws. His daughter has given him a grandson. As a native of Pittsburgh and an ex-Pirate, he keeps close to baseball and has close ties to both the Pirate and Cincinnati organizations. With the Reds, he pitched in three All-Star Games, hurled two games in the 1961 World Series, and had a 23–5 record in 1962. He's in both the Ohio Hall of Fame and the Cincinnati Reds' Hall of Fame.

A friend recently sent him a commemorative pin for the Dodgers' twenty-fifth anniversary in Dodger Stadium. Bob pitched and won the first game played there. He was also with the Pirates when the final games were played in both Ebbets Field and the Polo Grounds.

"At the Polo Grounds, we knew the fans were going to mob the field, and the clubhouse was in center field. I still remember that mad dash after the final out. We made it, but somebody has my cap from that day."

Because of his respected place in the business community of Bethel Park, Bob is well known as a former player and constantly is asked his opinions of baseball today. "It's your life—you never get away from it," he says with a smile. "People even think I'm supposed to be an expert on football."

RICK REICHARDT

BORN 1943
MINOR LEAGUES 1964–65
ANGELS 1964–70
SENATORS 1970
WHITE SOX 1971–73
ROYALS 1973–74

*R*ick Reichardt, the big, handsome bonus baby of the Los Angeles Angels in 1964, was swept away from football by the lure and love of baseball.

He had played in the 1963 Rose Bowl for the University of Wisconsin and led the Big Ten in receiving that year as a flanker back.

"My father was the Green Bay Packers' team doctor from 1955 to 1960," says Rick. "In fact, my best souvenir is a football autographed by the 1966 Packers, the first Super Bowl champions. Vince Lombardi had it sent to me after I had a kidney removed that year.

"I lost a lot of my baseball souvenirs," he says with a sigh. "I used to have people drive my car home to Wisconsin after the season when I was single. I'd want to go to Europe or something. This one year, the guy I trusted with the car stopped off in Las Vegas on the way. I guess he didn't do too well, because he hocked most of my things, including some special mementos, and left the car a mess."

Rick was the last of the big bonus players, for the following year the amateur-free-agent draft was instituted. It was reported that he received a $175,000 bonus.

"The tax laws were different then," says Rick, "and I really couldn't spread the payments out like they do today. I never really netted the kind of money people thought I had. But I'll tell you, if I had to do it over again, I'd have gone to the minors for a longer stretch and learned the game better. I don't think I really developed as a player until my last five years or so. I don't think I ever gave the Angels what I had in my later years, and I'm sorry about that because of the feeling I have for Gene Autry.

"I'll always consider myself a California Angel, no two ways about it. I hit the first home run in Anaheim Stadium and I still have an ongoing relationship with Mr. Autry. We exchange letters on a regular basis. I'll tell you one thing: Autry never—and I mean never—had a bad thing to say about anyone. He was always very supportive of the ball club and never interfered in the operation of the team. If he did stop by the clubhouse it was only to say hello or to pat some players on the back. You know, he and his wife never had any children of their own, and I think we were sort of their adopted children. So he's now got several hundred of us."

Although an Angel at heart, Rick readily admits his best years were spent with the White Sox. "Oakland was the dominant team in those days," he says, "but we always played them tough and came close to winning."

"My last year in baseball was 1974," he says, "and I decided the front office was right when I got released. Those people were probably good judges of my talent. I looked around for a while at several jobs. My college education, it turned out, really didn't prepare me for where I headed. I joined a life insurance company back in Wisconsin and worked for two years as an independent agent. Then I became my own boss. In 1981 I became a certified life underwriter and moved to Gainesville, Florida, because of the nice climate and living conditions. I opened Reichardt Enterprises, Inc., and I'm involved quite a bit with physicians' business interests.

"I'm also a partner with my three brothers in the restaurant business here, operating a string of Joe's Delis that are very popular, especially around the college campus."

Rick and his wife, Mary, live in a beautiful home in Gainesville with their three children, and he is very active with the Major League Baseball Players' Alumni Association. That keeps him in contact with many former players and gets him involved with a lot of Old Timers' Games.

"My kidney problems are all behind me now—I'm fine. I've just got to keep battling my weight. But things have worked out very well for me."

BOBBY RICHARDSON

BORN 1935
MINOR LEAGUES 1953–56
YANKEES 1955–66

*A*ll through his career with the Yankees, Bobby Richardson was well aware that his "milk-shake-drinking, Bible-reading" image might be a matter of some amusement to his teammates.

"Oh, I always knew they probably had some fun at my expense over it," says Bobby. "But the friendships I built there were genuine, and I always had the ability to laugh at myself a little, too.

"I don't get invited to the fantasy camps today because, as Whitey Ford told me, a lot of the week is spent in the cocktail lounge. He laughed when he told me, and so did I."

As proof of the sincerity of the friendships, Mickey Mantle and Joe DiMaggio flew to South Carolina in 1976 at their own expense to help Bobby campaign for Congress. Although he lost, he never forgot their gesture.

"A couple of years ago, Clete Boyer called and said he'd like to bring his family down and spend the Christmas holiday with us. I was never as close to Clete as I was to, say, Tony Kubek, but that was wonderful. We had a great time.

"When I retired, besides a gift from my teammates, Roger Maris bought me a beautiful watch, just from him, a special design. And Billy Martin, whose second-base job and uniform number were given to me, sent me a letter when his number was retired last year, telling me to always feel comfortable about wearing number one as long as I wanted to, at old timers' days and so forth. You'd never think, from our reputations, that Billy and I would be close, but he's always been great to me. Always."

Richardson retired from the Yankees after the 1966 season, at age thirty-one. He played one more year than he wanted so that both he and Kubek wouldn't retire together and leave the Yankees high and dry up the middle.

"Actually, Del Webb offered me sixty thousand dollars to play in 1967, which was fifteen thousand dollars over my top salary. I had a very unusual contract in those days, essentially a five-year deal. Webb said, 'Just tell me what you'll play for.'

"But I was retiring because of the travel. I wanted to go home and be with my family, and the money didn't matter. Lee MacPhail told me I could coach, manage the Triple A team, broadcast, or scout. I did some part-time scouting, but nothing that took me far from home."

After his young retirement, Bobby became a spokesman

for a life insurance company in South Carolina for three years and then became the baseball coach at the University of South Carolina. He built the baseball program into one of national recognition and coached the sons of Phil Rizzuto and Whitey Ford. But in 1976, persuaded by state Republican leaders, he ran for Congress. To prove the seriousness of his quest to voters, he resigned as baseball coach. Although he ran a good race, he lost. And his assistant having been promoted to head coach, he could not return to the Gamecocks.

"That was the campaign that Mantle and DiMaggio came down for," he says. "Steve Hamilton came down to be with Mantle, and we asked Tony Kubek to come down and be with DiMaggio. But Tony's politics were not in line with our conservative platform, and he turned me down. It hurt a little, but I understood. We have no problems today."

Bobby returned to coaching, but at small Bible schools, for small salaries. Columbia Bible College and its affiliated high school, the Ben Lippon School, employed him, before he moved on to Coastal Carolina College in 1984 for two seasons as athletic director and baseball coach.

In January 1987, former Giants' and Twins' pitcher Al Worthington resigned as baseball coach at Liberty University in Lynchburg, Virginia, to become the school's athletic director. Bobby was named to succeed him, and moved to Lynchburg.

"After all those years in Sumter, South Carolina, we're Virginians now," says Bobby, speaking of his wife, Betsy, and himself. Their five children are now grown.

Were they all model citizens in the Bobby Richardson tradition?

"More like the Betsy Richardson tradition," he says with a laugh. "Two of my boys became pastors, and my daughter married one. All five went to Christian colleges. I suppose we had some influence after all."

Coaching agrees with Bobby. As though to show his players how it's done, he had eight hits in nine at-bats during 1987 Old Timers' Games around the country.

BOB ROBERTSON

BORN 1946
**MINOR LEAGUES 1964–67,
1969**
**PIRATES 1967,
1969–76**
MARINERS 1978
BLUE JAYS 1979

*O*h, but to take back a single foul ball in a game that didn't even count.

"It was 1972, the year after my best season," says Bob Robertson, the broad-shouldered power hitter who patrolled first base for the world champion Pittsburgh Pirates of 1971. "There was a pop-up in Wrigley Field. I remember that it was a Game of the Week, and I remember the mud puddles along the running track, but I can't tell you who the hitter was. I went back for it, screwed up my knee, and was never the same again.

"The game was rained out after four innings and it didn't even count. I had never had a nosebleed all through youth leagues, school, the minors, no injuries at all from the game. And suddenly, one batted ball, and I was half a player."

The high point for Bob clearly was that 1971 season, when he hit twenty-six home runs in the regular season, and then a record four in the championship series against the Giants, including three in one game. He hit two more in the World Series comeback victory over the Orioles, best remembered for the great performance by Roberto Clemente.

"Clemente, he was an inspiration," says Robertson, now forty-one. "He'd always come up with something for you. Funny thing was, he was at his best when he was hurt. You'd hear him complaining about something and you knew he'd have a great day."

Although his knee would never be the same, Bob played on, remaining with the Pirates through the 1976 season. He went to spring training with the Pirates in 1977 but hurt his back and was released on March 31.

"I claimed it was a spring training injury, which it was, and they said it wasn't. It was in dispute. But I was released, and had a back operation, and then another one in 1980. But there are no hard feelings now. I feel close to the Pirate organization. I went back there for Old Timers' Day not long ago, just anxious to see if there was really something different about the baseball, with all the talk about the lively ball and all those home runs. The truth is, I really don't think it is the ball. Everybody today seems to swing with a big uppercut. No more Matty Alou types, no more hitting down on the ball like we were all taught in the Pirate organization. Of course, I never did get that down. I was always an uppercut-type hitter anyway."

When Bob retired, he opened an advertising business, B.

Robertson and Associates, which has an office in Somerset, Pennsylvania. "You do so much PR as a player, or at least you should, that it seemed a natural extension to get into PR or advertising. You think baseball will never stop, that it will go on forever, but one day you step into a mud puddle and you have to think about the future."

Bob lives with his wife and two daughters in LaVale, Maryland, not far from his birthplace of Frostburg. He also shares an interest with former Pirate pitcher Vern Law in a restaurant in Upper St. Clair, near Pittsburgh, "Vernon Law's Winning Steak," which opened in January 1987.

"We have 777 entrées to choose from," he says with a smile. It has nothing to do with his uniform, number seven, but there are also five sevens in his telephone number.

"I should have had a little seven on my knee that day in Wrigley, perhaps."

At his mother's home rests some of his prized souvenirs, including the ball he caught for the final out of the 1971 World Series, bats from all the Pirate regulars that year, the glove Donn Clendenon gave him when he turned over first base to Bob, Hank Aaron's 635th home run ("I just asked him for it"), and the MVP Award from the International League in 1969.

"What I miss most about baseball is the competition and the friendships," says Bob. "The money, that's all you hear about now, and that doesn't mean a thing to me. I'd love to get back in the game, even as a minor-league hitting instructor, and it wouldn't matter one bit what they paid. I was hoping the Pirates might have something for me when Syd Thrift became general manager—he first signed me— but I contacted him and he never called.

"Too many organizations hire superstars as coaches. I think it's a mistake. A guy like me, I knew what it was like to try and get out of a slump. I had plenty of them. There is a lot I could offer a young kid.

"For me, it was all about playing with Mays, Aaron, Banks, or standing in Yankee Stadium where Ruth and Mantle stood. Oh, I miss those days."

CARL SCHEIB

**BORN 1927
ATHLETICS 1943–45,
1947–54
MINOR LEAGUES 1955–57**

*H*is entry is on the very first page of *The Complete Baseball Record Book:*

YOUNGEST PLAYER, GAME

A.L.—16 years, 8 months, 5 days—Carl A. Scheib, Philadelphia, September 6, 1943, second game (pitcher).

If not for that, Carl would not be much remembered today. He was only a 45–65 lifetime pitcher, almost all of it for the forgettable Philadelphia Athletic teams from 1943 to 1954. But when he took the mound on that September day during World War II, he became the youngest player in major-league history.

A year later, Cincinnati's Joe Nuxhall, ten months younger, broke his record when he pitched for the Reds, but Scheib still is nestled comfortably in the record book with the American League mark. (He and Nuxhall have never met.)

"It wasn't a publicity gimmick," says Scheib today from his San Antonio, Texas, home. "In fact, there wasn't that much in the papers about it at all. It was a relief appearance, two innings, so you can't accuse Connie Mack of trying to build the gate with a stunt."

Scheib had been a high-school pitching star in Gratz, Pennsylvania. A salesman who serviced the local grocery store observed him pitching and wrote to Connie Mack about him.

"I don't remember the salesman's name, and I have no idea if he even knew Mr. Mack," recalls Scheib.

But the letter resulted in an invitation to Shibe Park (a coincidence), where Connie Mack, already a Hall of Famer but still managing, watched Carl pitch in the A's bullpen before a game. He was impressed enough to tell Carl to "keep in touch and look us up when you get out of school."

It had been Scheib's first trip out of Gratz. "I was so nervous about the trip, I even forgot my glove and shoes," he says.

But a year later, 1943, when school ended, Scheib did join the A's. He was not put on the roster, but he traveled with the team, pitching batting practice and getting comfortable with the company of big-leaguers.

After roster limits increased in September, Connie Mack asked, "You ready?" Scheib said he was, and Connie told him to get his father so he could sign a contract.

The day he signed was the day he made his historic appearance.

The right-hander pitched fifteen times in 1944, and four times in 1945, went off to military service in 1945 and 1946, and then took his regular turn with the A's starting rotation for the next seven years.

"Mr. Mack was pretty old then [he was born in 1862], and he wasn't very good with names anymore, but we all respected him a lot. There was no one who laughed at him behind his back or anything, even if he'd bump into you in an elevator and not remember who you were."

Scheib pitched in the majors into 1954 and wound up his career with three minor-league seasons. The 1954 season was the A's final one in Philadelphia before moving to Kansas City.

"My top salary was eleven thousand dollars. Times were hard then; it was hard to make ends meet. It wasn't so easy to get a winter job, either, because employers knew you'd only be available for a few months. But we all tried to get physical jobs to keep in shape. I think that made the players of my time stronger, although today's players are probably better conditioned, since they have the luxury of winters off and can get down to a good fitness program."

Scheib opened his own car wash/service station after his playing days, but after thirteen years decided he'd skip the headaches and work for someone else. He moved to Texas and continues to work for a company selling cleaning equipment and other items to car wash concerns.

He still gets letters from fans, but in San Antonio, few seem to care about his playing days. "I helped my son coach a Little League team a year ago," he said, "but no one on that team cared a bit about my once having been a major leaguer."

Scheib has little contact with teammates from his era. "I went to an Old Timers' Day in Philadelphia around 1980," he recalls, "and that was nice, but I'm really looking forward to going back to my high school team reunion this summer."

He sees Charlie Harris, an Athletic teammate from the late 1940s, once in a while, and his wife, Georgene, keeps in touch with the wives of ex-teammates Dick Fowler and Morrie Martin. Naturally, they kid each other about "the money we'd be making today."

Among his few souvenirs is the baseball from the game in which the A's set the record for double plays in one season (eventually 217 in 1949), which still stands today. It's signed by the regular infield of Hank Majeski, Eddie Joost, Pete Suder, and Ferris Fain.

Scheib plays tennis today and watches the Braves and Cubs a lot on cable TV. He has no special feeling for the A's, now twice removed from Philadelphia and playing in Oakland. He has a 1963 edition of the Turkin/Thompson *The Official Encyclopedia of Baseball* at home, and the Graig Nettles autobiography *Balls,* which someone gave him ("enjoyed it"), but as he turned sixty on New Year's Day 1987, Scheib might well have been just any ol' grandfather looking toward retirement and not living in the past at all.

"If I saw Connie Mack tomorrow, I'd just say, 'Thank you, Mr. Mack, for giving me the chance!' "

ENOS SLAUGHTER

BORN 1916
MINOR LEAGUES 1935–37
CARDINALS 1938–42,
1946–53
YANKEES 1954–55
ATHLETICS 1955–56
YANKEES 1956–59
BRAVES 1959

---

*E*nos "Country" Slaughter played until he was forty-three, in a time when players simply didn't do such things. The competitive drive that finally took him to the Hall of Fame still burns brightly at seventy-one.

Think Enos knows his lifetime stats without looking them up?

"No problem," he says with a drawl. "I went to bat 7,946 times, I played in 2,380 games, I had 2,383 hits, 413 doubles, 148 triples, 169 home runs, I had a lifetime average of

.300, scored 1,247 runs, drove in 1,304, had a .453 slugging percentage, I had 1,019 bases on balls, only struck out 538 times, I had a .980 fielding average, and 152 assists from the outfield."

Slaughter broke in with the Cardinals in 1938 and played for three owners there—Sam Breadon, Fred Saigh, and August Busch. "I was the first player Busch signed," he said, recalling the winter of 1953–54. "He told me, 'Enos, you're a credit to the game; you'll always be with me!' "

Two months later, he was traded to the Yankees. The newspapers all carried photos of Enos in tears.

"It broke my heart," he says. "They wanted to make room in the outfield for Wally Moon, but he couldn't have beaten me out of a job back then."

On the Yankees, Slaughter went to manager Casey Stengel and said he wanted a lot of playing time. "Casey said to me, 'My boy, you play when I want you to play and you'll be around a long time.' " He was right.

Slaughter's career ended in 1959. ("I wanted to be the first to play in four decades.") "Then in 1960, Marty Marion called and asked if I'd like to be playing manager at Houston, the Cardinals' Triple A farm club. I called him back a week later and accepted. Two hours later, the phone rang and I was offered a job as assistant radio announcer for the Baltimore Orioles. I might still be there today, but I couldn't take it. I gave my word to Marion."

In 1961, Slaughter managed Raleigh in the Carolina League for the Mets, who were to begin play the following season. "I ran fifty-four players through there for them, but we finished last, and that was the end of my career. I couldn't get back into baseball. I don't know if I was blackballed or what, but I never had another offer."

So Slaughter went home to North Carolina and his tobacco farm. In 1970 he was hired to coach baseball at Duke University, which he did for seven seasons. Since 1977, he's been back on his farm in Roxboro, his birthplace. He lives alone now after five marriages. He rises each day at 5:00 A.M. and can work until sundown on his plantings. "I work about four days and travel the other three, going to Old Timers' Games or celebrity golf tournaments," he says. "It keeps me young."

For a long time, Enos actively campaigned to get into the Hall of Fame before he was finally selected in 1985. Traces of bitterness remain. "The TV announcer Bob Costas was a sportswriter back in St. Louis, and wrote a column about me slipping in the back door or something. He said I didn't have the credentials. What was he, four when I quit playing?"

Slaughter also takes exception to the tough portrayal the Cardinals come under in accounts of 1947, Jackie Robinson's first season. "It's all a lie, that stuff about us threatening to strike and all," he says. "It was all made up by the New York writers. I always played hard, I always played to win. Red Barber wrote a book and said I intentionally stepped on Jackie and spiked him. Well, I did spike him, but it was because his foot was in the middle of the bag at first base. Didn't mean to. A couple of weeks later I put twenty-three stitches in [Bill] Rigney's hand at second base breaking up a play, but no one writes about that.

"Where I live today, there's not a white person for a mile around me—all colored and we get along fine."

Is Enos opinionated? Certainly. Is he a fantastic reminder of his time? Absolutely.

Cleveland Indians

AL SMITH

BORN 1928
MINOR LEAGUES 1948–53
INDIANS 1953–57
WHITE SOX 1958–62
ORIOLES 1963
INDIANS 1964
RED SOX 1964

"*T*hirty-five years ago," says Al Smith, "I was talking to a reporter in New York. The next day, I picked up his newspaper in the hotel. I read his story. It wasn't like anything I had said. And I haven't read a newspaper since."

He means it. He hasn't seen a sports section in thirty-five years. He hasn't shut baseball out of his life, but any connection between baseball and newspapers ended with that misquote in New York.

Today Smith keeps up with the game through television.

Even though he lives in Chicago, he's only been to about six games since his retirement.

"I don't like to get tangled in the crowd," he says.

When your name is Al Smith, it's indeed easy to get lost in a crowd. Al Smith is not exactly Van Lingle Mungo or Urbano Lugo. With a name like Al Smith, you need a good bat to get noticed. He had it. A lifetime .272 hitter who twice topped .300, he helped both the 1954 Indians and the 1959 White Sox to pennants, and he belted 164 home runs in his major-league career.

"That 1959 season, oh, that was fun," he says. "We were the 'Go-Go Sox,' and every day was fun. I think I won about ten or eleven games with homers that year."

In fact, he hit seventeen for the Sox that year, with the rest of the team hitting only eighty more.

Another special memory, however, is reserved for the 1954 Indians. Al was twenty-six, in only his first full season in the majors. His ball club won a record 111 games that year, which amazingly still stands, even with expansion and a schedule of eight extra games that has now existed for more than a quarter century. Al scored 101 runs for the Indians that year, and then in 1955 he led the league with 123 while batting .306.

His common link between the Indians and the White Sox was manager Al Lopez, the only man to win pennants in the 1950s in the American League besides Casey Stengel. (Lopez won two.) Lopez had his favorites, and Smith was one of them.

Al spent five and a half years in the minors before he hit the big time, so his first year of organized ball, 1948, came just a year after Jackie Robinson's entry into the majors. It made him one of the pioneers in breaking the color barrier.

"I eventually got up to a top salary of fifty-eight thousand dollars," he says, "and I didn't throw it around. I ran the baseball program for the Chicago Parks Department for fifteen years, then we moved to Tucson, Arizona.

"We still have that place, but we came back to Chicago when my wife's mother passed three years ago. We needed to look after her property. My wife used to work for the airlines, so we still travel a lot, Las Vegas, California, you name it. We do all right."

A grandfather nine times over, Al will occasionally pull out some old photos to share with the children. One of them is a shot from the 1959 World Series, when a fan spilled a cup of beer over Al as he ran back to the wall chasing down a home run.

"Yeah, that one got a lot of attention," he says with a laugh. "I didn't like giving up the home run, but I had to smile over the beer. What else could you do?"

Al will see his old mentor Al Lopez from time to time in Chicago or Florida, and the two remain good friends. "He's a good man," is the Smith assessment of the man who helped him into two World Series. "He had confidence in me, and I came through for him."

DARYL SPENCER

BORN 1929
MINOR LEAGUES 1949–52
GIANTS 1952–53,
  1956–59
CARDINALS 1960–61
DODGERS 1961–63
REDS 1963
JAPAN 1964–68,
  1971–72

"*T*here's a cable television show here in Wichita," explains Daryl Spencer, "called *Time Out for Trivia*. I always try to get through on the phones to ask the host a question. If I ever do get through, my question would be: 'Who hit the first home run on the West Coast?' The answer is me. I hit one on Opening Day in 1958 off Don Drysdale."

Spencer laughs at the tidbit. He knows he sounds like a fan.

"Here's another one," he says. "On May 12 and 13, 1959,

Willie Mays and I hit back-to-back home runs. I don't know if any two guys ever hit back-to-backers two straight days."

Daryl's enjoying this. He's very pleased with the memories. He's also proud of still holding the Giants' record for home runs and RBIs in one season by a shortstop (seventeen and seventy-four, respectively). "I also held the second-base record until Tito Fuentes broke it," he adds.

Daryl Spencer was a hard-nosed infielder in the 1950s when a player had to scrap to hold on to his job. "When I played, there was no such thing as a disabled list," he says. "It really bothers me to see a poor effort displayed by a ballplayer. When I played, there were three or four Pete Roses on every team. Nowadays it's rare to see one."

The analogy is interesting, for Spencer finished up in the majors playing third base at Cincinnati in Pete Rose's rookie season at second base.

"My most memorable moment," Spencer says, really getting into it now, "was in 1952 at the old Polo Grounds. It was when I took the field for the first time as a major leaguer and realized my lifelong dream. Tears filled my eyes as I thought of my dad. He died while I was in high school, and he couldn't be with me to see my dream fulfilled. I remember playing catch with him when I was five, six years old. Even then I thought about maybe being a big leaguer someday.

"The Giants and the Dodgers—what a great rivalry that was. Especially back in 1953 when Leo Durocher was managing the Giants. There was always some kind of controversy. Every series you knew there was going to be a knockdown deal. Every game you knew you would have at least one or two knockdown pitches. Now when you watch a game and a player gets knocked down, you have some type of arbitration."

"When my career in the majors ended," he says, "I went to Japan as a player for five seasons. I played for the Hankyo Braves. After that I went into the restaurant franchise business, just as it was getting popular. But it didn't work out for me, and I went back to Japan in 1971 for two seasons as a player-coach. One thing I learned in Japan was the importance of concentration. It was so obvious that the .300 hitters were the guys who were always into the game all the time.

"After those two seasons, I came home and got involved coaching semipro ball. We won two state titles in five years."

Spencer still works today, running a warehouse in Wichita, his birthplace. One daughter lives nearby, another is in Oklahoma City.

"I never saved a lot of stuff," he says, "but I do have a New York Giants' road uniform and a couple of valuable unused tickets—one from the first game on the West Coast—the one I hit that home run off Drysdale in—and one from the third game of the 1954 World Series. Unfortunately, I was in the service and missed out on that. I missed again in '62 when the Giants beat the Dodgers in a playoff; I was with the Dodgers then. And I missed in '63 when the Dodgers traded me to Cincinnati and they went on to win.

"Never mind the souvenirs," he says. "It's the memories that count. I played with Mays, Musial, Koufax, Drysdale, Frank Robinson, all those great Hall of Famers."

New York Mets

RON SWOBODA

BORN 1944
MINOR LEAGUES 1964
METS 1965–70
EXPOS 1971
YANKEES 1971–73

*D*escribing himself as "funky and unstructured," Ron Swoboda is comfortable and at home as a television sports reporter in New Orleans. The fact that he works in a nonmajor-league town is a tribute to his having achieved success in this industry on his own merits and not on the glamour his name once held for legions of New York Mets fans.

Ironically, Swoboda wound up in an industry where he has packed up his family and moved more than he did in baseball. To be a serious broadcaster, it goes with the territory.

"I went to spring training with the Braves in 1974," he says, describing his postbaseball life. "It was the spring Henry Aaron was set to break Babe Ruth's home run record. I never saw anyone handle such media attention so easily. When he broke the record, I was watching on TV. It was the most amazing thing I'd ever seen. So cool."

The Braves cut Swoboda, and he went back home to Long Island, New York, where he'd established roots during his Met and Yankee playing days. Soon Bill MacPhail, the head of CBS Sports, called and offered him the opportunity to do the sports reports for WCBS-TV in New York, the network's flagship station. He did that for four years, then went to WISN in Milwaukee for two, where "I was something less than a success." Next stop, New Orleans. There he found his groove as a broadcaster. "If it felt right, I went with it," he says. The stay at WVUE was a happy one, but a change in management brought a change in on-air talent, and Swoboda was off again, this time for KTVK in Phoenix. "It was twice the money, but it was a difficult place for me to work. I was thrilled to be able to return to WVUE in 1987. I can see myself running out the string in New Orleans."

With two grown boys, Swoboda, at only forty-three, is young to be alone at home with his wife. But he's looking forward to it. "My maturity and emotions have always been a little behind where they should have been at a given age," he says. "I think I'm finally where I should be."

No doubt some of that could be from playing the game that Roy Campanella said required "a lot of little boy in you." Swoboda was a major leaguer at twenty, after only 139 minorleague games. He was, perhaps, "the next Mickey Mantle" to be broken in by Casey Stengel when he joined the hapless Mets in 1965.

"I didn't really know all about Casey until I read Bob Creamer's biography of him just last year," says Ron. "But he had a fabulous mind and treated me really good. He was born of entirely different stock, came through such hard times, and was a survivor. He had a face like Mount Rushmore, but his blue eyes would dance, and if he spotted you across the room, he'd begin telling the writers a story that he wanted you to hear, some lesson about baseball he wanted you to learn."

Swoboda's friends remain important to him, especially ones he made from his New York days. "I had friends among the ball-park police, the blue-collar types, and then I made a little money and moved to Syosset, where everyone else was maybe ten years older than me and very white-collar. But they accepted me, brought me into their fold. We had a book club—we'd all read the same books, like *The World According to Garp*, or *Shōgun*, and then we'd discuss them together. Fascinating people. I cried when I left them all to move to Milwaukee. It was the first time I cried since I was a high school senior, when I wasn't playing baseball very well, and I stood in the outfield and began to think about all the summers I'd wasted for nothing trying to be a ball-player."

Unlike many major leaguers who are superstars from Little League on, Swoboda was not a natural or gifted athlete. He was often not the best player on his team in youth leagues. But he worked hard to earn what he got, including a contract with the Mets after a year at the University of Maryland.

"When I visit my mom in Baltimore," he says, "I sleep in my old bed, and all the Little League trophies are still there, next to it."

His major-league memories are in "unclipped condition," but his wife saved many pages, and "maybe when we get old, we'll clip them nicely and put them in a scrapbook."

Foremost in his memory, of course, is the 1969 World Series, in which he batted .400 for the "Miracle Mets" and made one of the great catches in Series history, a diving grab on a sinking liner off the bat of Brooks Robinson.

"That I have on tape. Each time we've moved I've hung up less and less of the baseball plaques and photos. I don't know if I'll hang up the photo of that catch again, but it is a special memory."

To have been a '69 Met was to have been part of one of the select teams of destiny, of countless books, of classic baseball lore.

"I get a warm feeling about that team, especially if we're together at a reunion or something. Most of 'em were good guys. Remember, we were thrown together, we didn't choose each other. And then it all happened for us, and we're forever linked in history. Thank goodness for the opportunity."

FRANK THOMAS

BORN 1929
MINOR LEAGUES 1948–52
PIRATES 1951–58
REDS 1959
CUBS 1960–61
BRAVES 1961
METS 1962–64
PHILLIES 1964–65
ASTROS 1965
BRAVES 1965
CUBS 1966

*F*rank Thomas spent parts of sixteen seasons in the big leagues, mostly with his first team, the Pittsburgh Pirates, but it is the New York Mets who conjure up many of his most vivid memories, even though he spent only two and half years with them.

"I would say I follow the Mets the closest," he says from his home in Pittsburgh, not far from the place where he was born in 1929. "The Mets' organization was great to me over the years. I've played in sixteen Mets' Old Timers' Day games, and I go to their fantasy camp. Last year, in fact, I played twenty-four innings in one day at the camp. I'm still in pretty good shape.

"The '62 original Mets were an amazing bunch. Casey Stengel was one of a kind. He probably forgot more baseball than I'll ever know. You know, although we lost a multitude of games that first season [120], we never went out on the field with a losing attitude. We weren't as bad as we seemed. In fact, we lost many games in the seventh, eighth, or ninth innings by one run."

Thomas hit 34 home runs for the '62 Mets, which stood as a team record until Dave Kingman broke it in 1975.

"I played professional baseball for eighteen years," says Thomas, "and twelve of those seasons were spent with last-place clubs. But I'll tell you one thing: I always gave 100 percent of my God-given ability and didn't care what people said as long as I gave an honest effort."

"I still see many former teammates," he adds, "and the stories grow bigger and bigger each year. Most guys become .350 hitters over the years."

Thomas retired after the 1966 season with 286 career home runs. As the father of eight children (one now deceased) it was time to go to work.

"I began to walk the streets looking for a job," he recalls. "I wound up working for the ICM School of Business. I worked there for eighteen years before retiring just a few years ago. My job was to go to various high schools and speak about education to the kids. I would always tell them that if you do play sports—any sport—you may be around until you're maybe thirty-seven if you are very lucky. That means you have twenty-eight years left until you're sixty-five, retirement age. I emphasize that education is essential."

Thomas, who studied for the priesthood before entering

professional baseball, is a man of great pride in his past and still very caught up with the world of baseball. He loves the invitations to the old timers' gatherings and the fantasy camps, and loves getting together with old friends like Bill Mazeroski, Bob Purkey, Roy Face, and Bob Friend at golf tournaments.

"I saved a lot of stuff from my playing days," he says. "I have uniforms from the Pirates and Mets. I have bats from the three All-Star Games I played in, 1954, 1955, and 1958. There are baseballs in my family room from various milestones, like my first hit [1951], my hundredth home run [1956], and my two-hundredth homer [1961]. I also have two baseballs that I cherish a great deal. A minor-league umpire named George Sosnak took these two balls and hand-designed all types of information about my career on them. They're amazing."

"Fans still write, and kids still come around for autographs. I take them into my family room and show them the memorabilia, and they ask me questions about being a ballplayer. I always tell them how much I really enjoyed playing the game."

New York Yankees

RUSTY TORRES

BORN 1948
MINOR LEAGUES 1967–72
YANKEES 1971–72
INDIANS 1973–74
MINOR LEAGUES 1975
ANGELS 1976–77
MINOR LEAGUES 1978
WHITE SOX 1978–79
MINOR LEAGUES 1980
ROYALS 1980

"One day a couple of years ago," says Rosendo "Rusty" Torres, "I was working sanitation in Long Island, and what do you know, Whitey Ford is on my route. Every day I'm collecting Whitey Ford's garbage. Well, I knew him from spring training with the Yankees, when he was a coach, so I left a note in his mailbox saying it was me picking up his garbage.

"He never called, though. I'll bet he remembered the time I hit a foul ball in Fort Lauderdale and it smashed the windshield of his 1939 Ford Replica."

Rusty laughs. He always had a good laugh and was a good man on a ball club. He kept people loose and made them laugh. He's very likable. But there have been few laughs for Rusty in recent years.

"I finished up with Kansas City in 1980," he says. "I was there when George Brett was hitting .400. That was amazing to watch. But that was the end of the line. I got released the day before I would have been eligible for a World Series. It would have been my only one.

"But I kept trying to catch on here and there, just to stay in shape in case a call came. I even went down to the Dominican Republic where they have a summer league, not the good winter league that you hear about. A summer league where they pay about seventy-five dollars a month. But that was as far as I was going to go."

Rusty, a native of Puerto Rico who was raised streetwise in New York, returned to New York with his wife and four children, looking for work. Nothing was coming up. He sold the World Series ring the Royals sent him and used his half share to pay bills. But he was pretty much broke. His car was stolen, and he hadn't been able to pay his insurance bills on it, so it was a total loss.

"I couldn't buy my kids a pair of pants," he says.

Then one day he was arrested. He was charged with selling drugs.

"It was two weeks after the same thing happened to Joe Pepitone," he says. "Not a good time for ex-Yankees."

He avoided jail by pleading guilty to the felony and was placed on five years' probation and three hundred hours of community service.

"I was in the backseat and I was drunk," he says. "I was getting a ride to my father's house in Queens. It was said that I was paid thirty dollars and a half gram to be a bodyguard. I had nothing to do with a drug sale. But my lawyer told me to plead guilty to avoid prison."

The felony conviction set Rusty back even farther. A job was harder to land. They couldn't keep their apartment. His wife of twenty-two years had to move in with her parents in Brooklyn; Rusty moved in with his in Queens. His son joined the Air Force, a daughter works for the city, two younger ones are with his wife.

"I'm bilingual, I get along well with people, I'll do anything—sanitation, mail room, anything. I'm out in the streets looking for a future."

"My family's been great to me. I make a little money selling autographed pictures in my Yankee uniform. I'm six years away from being able to collect a pension."

Torres was voted the best rookie in spring training with the 1971 Yankees, but in 1972 he was traded to the Cleveland Indians in the deal that brought Graig Nettles to New York.

"Four of us went in the trade," he says, "and all four of us had won the watch for being the best rookie at one time or another."

"The saddest thing was the Kansas City experience. I hadn't played in months when I signed to play at Omaha. In eight games I hit .360, and the Royals called me up. I wasn't ready. I was so out of shape. First game was in Yankee Stadium. I was in right field and a ball is hit to me. On one play, I pulled a leg muscle and sprained my arm. I was useless the rest of the way. Jim Frey thought I was jaking it, I'm sure.

"I've taken my dad to Yankee Stadium a few times. We sit in the back. I'd sort of like to tell people that I once played there, but . . ."

At thirty-nine, with a head of white hair and an uncertain

future, baseball was a long way in Rusty's past. Yet there's still a twinkle in his eye and that likable smile on his face. Somehow this survivor of the baseball travails that are inflicted on the journeymen—all those trips to the minors, all those last-minute cuts in spring training—seems as though he's going to pull this one out, get back on his feet, and bring that easy nature into a rewarding future. He's an optimist.

National Baseball Hall of Fame

CECIL TRAVIS

**BORN 1913
MINOR LEAGUES 1931–33
SENATORS 1933–41,
1945–47**

---

*C*ecil Travis played the in-
field for the Washington Senators for a dozen years, mostly
during the Great Depression.

"To tell you the truth," he recalls, "I think Washington
was a little better off than other cities during the Depression. It was a government town, and government workers
had jobs. So they could come out and watch us play. On the
other hand, most of them were from out of town, and they'd
come and root for their hometown team rather than us.
Usually, more were rooting for the visitors than for us."

Travis's rookie season was also the rookie season for Franklin D. Roosevelt in the White House.

"Imagine that, me, a farm boy from Georgia, and I got to play in front of presidents. Roosevelt, then Truman, they'd come to our Opening Days. I never caught a first ball, but I still remember all the excitement."

Travis was quite a hitter for a shortstop, hitting a career .314 with a high of .359 in 1941. He had five hits in his 1933 debut. But as luck would have it, his peak coincided with the Second World War, and he was off to service until late in the 1945 season.

"You never think about what you lost," he says. "We had a job to do, an obligation, and we did it. I was hardly the only one."

Most of his service time was spent in the States, but in the end he spent ten months with the 76th Infantry Division fighting in Belgium and Germany.

"When I returned, I was thirty-two and had been away for almost four seasons, so I wasn't the player I had been. But that was okay. Everything was okay. I have no regrets about anything. Maybe I could have made more money playing for a different team, but Mr. Griffith wasn't a rich man, and I can't complain."

Clark Griffith, the Hall of Fame owner of the Senators and a nineteenth-century pitching star, "never missed anything. He was very observant. He'd be at every game. After all, this was his life. He didn't have another business. He was a good man, but he could be rough on contracts. He'd handle all the negotiations himself, and you'd argue for the longest time over two hundred or three hundred dollars."

After Travis retired in 1947, he scouted for the Senators for five years. "Those were the days when you'd find a prospect, but you'd have to outbid other clubs. We didn't have the money to outbid them, so a lot of guys got away. I finally gave it up to go back to the farm."

"The farm" was a family property, which at the time covered 450 acres and had seventy-five head of cattle, raised for beef. It was twelve miles outside Atlanta, on Route 138 in Riverdale. That is where Travis, now seventy-four, lives with his wife of forty-five years and one of their three sons.

"We have just a few cattle now, on sixty-five acres. That's how we made the farm profitable: not by selling beef, but by selling off the land. Property values keep going up. I get only a small baseball pension."

Travis and his son are the only ones who tend to the farming, but his health is good and he has plenty of time to follow baseball.

"The Braves have sent me a season pass ever since they came down here in 1966," he says. "I don't know who's responsible, but they've just been great about it. I used to go more often, but now the traffic getting downtown is awful."

Travis also gave up Old Timers' Games several years ago. "I didn't want to take a chance on getting killed," he says sincerely. "I mean it—one of these days one of those players in an Old Timers' Game is going to get killed. You've got to play this game every day to handle it."

"I still have my old mitt," he says, "but I haven't picked up a baseball in years."

Jim Turner (left)
with ex-pupil Bob Turley

JIM TURNER

BORN 1903
MINOR LEAGUES 1925–36
BRAVES 1937–39
REDS 1940–42
MINOR LEAGUES 1942
YANKEES 1942–45
MINOR LEAGUES 1946–47

*F*or a fellow who threw his first professional pitch six weeks before Lou Gehrig began his record playing streak in 1925, Jim Turner is remarkably hale and hearty at eighty-four. A shoulder replacement operation in 1984 forced him to give up golf, but he gets more than his share of exercise in Nashville, Tennessee.

"In my backyard," he says, "if I walk a figure eight sixteen times, it's a mile. I walk a lot. I also mow the lawns, and occasionally go eighteen miles out to the little farm we rent out and do some work with a chain saw."

Turner has outlived most of his teammates on the 1937 Boston Braves, for whom he won twenty as a thirty-four-year-old rookie and led the league with a 2.38 earned-run average. He's even outlived his three younger fellow coaches on the Yankees in the late 1960s and early 1970s—Jim Hegan, Elston Howard, and Dick Howser.

"Those were terrible tragedies," he says. "Really fine people, nice fellows. It's funny how life goes."

Turner remains sharp of mind and an avid fan, and each season he purchases five season tickets to watch the Nashville Sounds of the American Association, now a Reds' farm. He attends about 90 percent of their games.

Ironically, when the Nashville franchise was operated by the Reds and was part of the Southern League in 1960, Jim was given the job as manager and general manager.

"I was pitching coach of the Yankees from 1949 to 1959," he recalls, with no hint of bitterness. "In the first five years, we won five world championships. In 1954, we were second, but won 103 games. Then we won four more pennants in a row. In 1959, we finished third. And George Weiss decided not to renew my contract. Fortunately, Gabe Paul, who was operating the Reds, gave me the job in Nashville, and after one season, I was made the Reds' pitching coach."

At Cincinnati, Turner was on hand for the debut of Pete Rose, "just a skinny kid then, but a real example of what you can do with yourself even if you have only average abilities." He coached for the Reds for five years, then rejoined the Yankees when Ralph Houk asked him back in 1966. He stayed with Houk until Ralph resigned in 1973, then went to spring training with the Tigers in 1974, Houk's first year there.

"That was enough," he says with a laugh. "Longest seven weeks of my life. Steve Hamilton was the new pitching coach and Ralph wanted me to help out, but it was time to retire. I knew it."

Turner pitched, of course, when starting pitchers were measured by durability as well as ability. "It was expected," he says, "that your first three starting pitchers would be complete-game pitchers, and the fourth man would require some bullpen assistance. Now I see only a handful of men—like Blyleven, Valenzuela, and Clemens—who work with nine innings in mind and hold their stuff for all nine. But the minor leagues train men to pitch relief these days, so it makes sense."

As for the split-finger fastball, made popular today by the teaching of Roger Craig, Turner says, "It's really just an old forkball. Lindy McDaniel threw it. Roy Face threw it. The first one I ever saw throw it was Myles Thomas, who was on the 1927 Yankees. I saw him pitch it with Los Angeles in the Pacific Coast League in 1930. I never threw it myself."

In his den, Turner proudly shows off a tiny little black mitt he used in 1929, 1930, and 1931, when he won sixty-seven games at Greensboro and Hollywood, where he first saw Thomas pitch. He doesn't make a fuss about his souvenirs, but he's mighty proud of original uniforms from the '37 Braves and the '40 Reds as well as a couple of hundred signed baseballs. One is from the only home run he ever hit, back in 1939 with the Braves. "But I lost the game, 3–2, to Hugh Mulcahy of the Phillies." Turner also has signed baseballs from two of his pennant-winning years as a player: 1940 (with the Reds) and 1942 (with the Yankees).

He lives with his two unmarried daughters, one a high school chemistry teacher and basketball coach, and the other a pediatrician with the Tennessee State Health Department. The year 1986 marked his sixtieth wedding anniversary. He won't subscribe to cable TV because "I don't like the movies they show," but he watches whatever games the networks offer, with a special interest in teams he's familiar with, like the Yankees or Sparky Anderson's Tigers. And you can count on him as a renewal customer for his Nashville season tickets for next season, he insists.

Don Wingfield

JOSÉ VALDIVIELSO

BORN 1934
MINOR LEAGUES 1953–59
SENATORS/TWINS 1955–56,
 1959–61
MINOR LEAGUES 1962–64

---

*T*o be a utility infielder on the
Washington Senators during a decade in which last place
was their usual finish: Could there have been a lower rung
on the major-league ladder?

"Low rung?" asks José Valdivielso, "I never thought of
it. I was so happy to be in the majors; so many wonderful
people there. What an opportunity! The best years of
my life!"

In truth, José played only 401 major-league games—325
with the Senators, and 76 with the Minnesota Twins when

the franchise moved. He hit .219, with nine home runs.

"I got up to seventy-five hundred dollars a year," he says with a laugh, "but when we moved to Minnesota, we heard that Calvin Griffith doubled the salaries of his whole family, which was the front-office staff. That meant he had to find someone to play shortstop for less than me. So he got Zoilo Versalles, who went on to win an MVP award."

Valdivielso, known even to his Latin friends as Joe, came up from Cuba in 1953. "The Senators had Joe Cambria as a scout," he says, "and he saved the franchise. He had once owned the Havana Cubans, and now he scouted the island for Mr. Griffith. I was playing sandlot ball with people like Sandy Amoros, Camilo Pascual, Pedro Ramos, Mike Fornieles, Carlos Paula, and Willy Miranda. Cambria signed a lot of us for the Senators.

"I'd been a big fan of pro ball in Cuba, listening to Buck Canel describe the games on the radio, as we all did."

José reached the majors in 1955, around the time Harmon Killebrew was coming along. "He had to sit in the majors for two years because of the bonus rule," recalls Joe, "and it was hard for him at the beginning. But when he came back, oh, what shots he hit!"

Valdivielso recalls Clark Griffith late in his life: "We were in Orlando at Tinker Field for spring training, and Mr. Griffith must have been eighty-three or eighty-four. They were pretty relaxed about smoking in spring training then, believe it or not, and he saw me smoking a cigarette near the dugout. He came over and said, 'José?'—I was amazed he knew me—'you should not smoke. Watch the game! Learn your trade!'

"The most amazing thing was, the next spring, he remembered the incident and reminded me of it. What a wonderful man he was."

"It was sad to leave Washington for Minnesota," says José, "and sometimes if I'm in Washington, I go by where old Griffith Stadium was. Only buildings are there now. I wouldn't trade the memories for anything. I wish I had some of my mementos from those days, but I had to leave everything in Cuba."

José married a New Yorker, and when his career ended he moved to New York and was a salesman for an electrical supply company for a few months. Then he became a supervisor for neighborhood youth groups in the New York City Mission Society. "New York is a great place to work if you're bilingual," he notes. He became a sales supervisor for Bustelo Coffee, and he learned the broadcasting business, giving baseball scores on Spanish radio stations, and then, coincidentally, becoming a broadcast partner with the famed Buck Canel, doing Yankee games for Latin America and Spanish radio.

"Buck, what a man," says José. "I'm so glad he was selected to the Hall of Fame. Everyone from Latin America, from the 1930s to the 1980s, knew his voice like their own father's. What a wonderful teacher he was to me."

Now José uses his talents to produce his own sports segment on Spanish television in the New York area, at WNJU, and to sell the commercial time accompanying it. He is a familiar figure on the New York sports scene, but not many know he used to play the infield for the Senators.

Married thirty-two years and a grandfather twice over, José lives comfortably on Long Island, a long way from Matanzas, Cuba, and the sandlots that took him to Washington.

ELMER VALO

BORN 1921
MINOR LEAGUES 1939–41
ATHLETICS 1940–43,
  1946–56
PHILLIES 1956
DODGERS 1957–58
MINOR LEAGUES 1959
INDIANS 1959
YANKEES 1960
SENATORS/TWINS 1960–61
PHILLIES 1961

*E*lmer Valo was not only the last major leaguer from Czechoslovakia, he also was the last major leaguer named Elmer.

But we can do better than that.

If Elmer had been a Broadway show, he would be known as the man who closed three cities.

He had the unique distinction of playing for the Philadelphia Athletics when that franchise transferred to Kansas City after the 1954 season; of playing for the Brooklyn Dodgers when Ebbets Field shut its doors and the Dodgers moved to Los Angeles after the 1957 season; and of playing for the Washington Senators in 1960 and moving with them to Minnesota.

"Yes," he says laughingly, "it must have been me."

In fact, Valo, hardly remembered as one of the "Boys of Summer," had the game-winning RBI in the final Ebbets Field game, doubling home a first-inning run while batting third in the lineup.

"I was with the Athletics for fifteen years," he says, "so naturally, my fondest memories are with them. But after them would come the Dodgers. They were a wonderful organization."

Elmer, indeed, would be a good judge of such things. After the fifteen-year run with the A's, he spent the last six years of his career wearing the uniforms of the Phillies, Dodgers (in two cities), Seattle Rainiers (in the Pacific Coast League), Indians, Yankees, Senators/Twins, and finally the Phillies again. For his twenty seasons of service in the big leagues, he hit .282, topping .300 five times.

"Heck, I have no idea what my final average was—around .280, I suppose. I get about four or five letters a day from fans, some with old baseball cards, and they have the records on the back. But I was never one for records. I was always just proud and happy to have a job."

After his playing days, Elmer strung together a long career as a coach and scout, mostly with the Phillies, as his ties to the Philadelphia area remained strong. He scouted in the Northeast for the Phillies for many years before retiring in 1982.

"Scouting became very different after the draft began in 1965," he explains. "You could discover someone, but it was hard to keep it secret, and some other organization would select him ahead of you. Plus, so much of the talent really began to come from California."

Valo himself came to this country when he was six, so he learned baseball at the same time as American-born boys and was never really thought of as a "foreign" player. He signed with the Athletics at eighteen, in 1939.

"Mr. Mack was like a guiding light to me," he recalls, speaking of Athletics' manager Connie Mack. "No one ever called him Connie to his face. Maybe we'd use it talking about him among ourselves, but I never saw one player call him Connie."

Valo adds, "His coaches, Al Simmons, Jimmie Dykes, Lena Blackburne, they were also like father figures. Real good people."

A bad back ended his ability to swing a bat and helped bring about his retirement. But he still goes to Clearwater in the spring at the Phillies' invitation to help at spring training, which keeps him close to the game. He and his wife of forty-six years, Anna, have five grandchildren, and "the older ones are like other young fans, always asking me a lot of baseball questions. I love it. But I ran out of pictures a while ago, so I can't really accommodate the neighborhood kids anymore."

Valo's good friends from his playing days were Pete Suder, Hank Majeski, Buddy Rosar, and Alex Kellner, with whom he still keeps in touch. He says he lives comfortably, and adds, "Thank goodness for the pension plan." His top salary was in the low thirty thousands for a couple of years.

In recent years Elmer, with more free time on his hands, spends time in his local library in Palmerton, Pennsylvania, where he has sat and read such books as Graig Nettles' *Balls* and Frank Deford's *The World's Tallest Midget*.

"When I played," Valo says, "there weren't many baseball books intended for adults. And they sure weren't like these."

HARRY WALKER

BORN 1918
MINOR LEAGUES 1937–41
CARDINALS 1940–43,
  1946–47
PHILLIES 1947–48
CUBS 1949
REDS 1949
MINOR LEAGUES 1950–58
CARDINALS 1950–51,
  1955
MANAGER, CARDINALS 1955
MANAGER, PIRATES 1965–67
MANAGER, ASTROS 1968–72

*H*arry Walker could hit. He could hit as a player, and he could teach the skill to others. He probably could still hit today.

"I spent forty-two years in the game," he says, "and I am always thinking about my days in baseball. Even now, I'm almost sixty-nine, and I'm still a great fan. I travel now and then just to see various clubs play. I was there when Don Sutton won his three-hundredth and I was there when Tom Seaver won his three-hundredth. I've been to Fenway, the Vet, and Arlington Stadium just recently."

Harry and his brother Dixie, another fine hitter, who died in 1982, were the sons of a pitcher named Dixie Walker, who hurled for the Senators from 1909 to 1912.

"I've got a picture of my dad with his roommate Walter Johnson," says Harry, who was also called "The Hat" for his habit of wearing them so often. "But I've got plenty of my own stuff, too. Many pictures, World Series rings. I'll tell you what I have; in 1941, I used the first two-tone-colored bat. In fact, Louisville Slugger now has it in their line—the Walker Finish, they call it."

Born in Pascagoula, Mississippi, in 1918, Harry now speaks from his fifty-acre spread in Leeds, Alabama. He lives across from a country club he helped found, and on which they stage a Harry Walker Golf Tournament each year.

"I'm really enjoying my life at this time," he says. "To tell you the truth, I'm making more money now than I ever have. I'm quite independent and am having a great time."

Harry won the 1947 batting championship in the National League, hitting .363 after being traded by the Cardinals to the Phillies in April. His major-league career effectively ended in 1950, but he continued to use his batting skills as a player-coach or player-manager through 1958. He began managing in 1951, and he had his last managing assignment with the Houston Astros from 1968 to 1972.

"After I finished as a player in the majors, I led the American Association with a .393 average as playing manager in 1951 at Columbus. The next year, at Rochester, I hit .365."

"After I managed at Houston, I went back to St. Louis for six years as a batting instructor. After that I worked with Jack Buck in the radio booth for one year, doing color commentary. Then I moved to the front office, where I was involved in trade decisions and player personnel moves. After six years, however, I got tired of the travel and the pace of the game. It was time to retire for good. But I'm still at the University of Alabama-Birmingham, where I'm the assistant to the athletic director, so I'm still involved in the game."

Ever the batting instructor, Harry wrote a book on hitting in 1959, and he currently has a videotape out called *Harry Walker on Hitting,* which is used by many colleges and some professional organizations as well.

"From what I see today, Wade Boggs has the ideal touch," says Harry, "with Tony Gwynn and Don Mattingly not far behind. The best player, in terms of combining the five important elements of the game—speed, average, running, throwing, and fielding—was Joe DiMaggio. No question."

"I miss baseball dearly today, and if I could do it all over again, I'd absolutely love it. We won a pennant my first year in the majors, and we won 106 games, then beat the Yankees in five games in the World Series. I hit .314 that year. What a way to break in.

"The year I was traded to the Phillies I felt terrible, but I won the batting title by forty-six points.

"By the way, my brother led the league in hitting one year with a .357 average, and I believe we are the only brothers to lead the league in hitting.

"Baseball today is very different from when I played," he adds. "The big thing is the closeness of the players. In my time, we went everywhere by train. Sometimes we would be on a train for twenty-four to thirty hours at at time. We would talk baseball more. We lived it more."

Harry still lives it, although from a distance. He has it in his blood.

Houston Astros

DANNY WALTON

BORN 1947
MINOR LEAGUES 1965–69
ASTROS 1968
PILOTS/BREWERS 1969–71
YANKEES 1971
MINOR LEAGUES 1971–72
TWINS 1973, 1975
MINOR LEAGUES 1974–75
DODGERS 1976
MINOR LEAGUES 1976–80
ASTROS 1977
MINOR LEAGUES 1979
RANGERS 1980

---

*E*very now and then, Danny Walton allows his mind to slip back to that summer's day in 1970. When he awoke in the morning, he was on top of the world. He "owned" Milwaukee. Coulda been elected mayor. The Brewers were in their first season; baseball had returned after the Braves' unceremonious departure five years earlier. The fans were falling in love with these new major-league heroes, and Danny Walton was the biggest of 'em all.

He had gotten off to a terrific start. He had been on the cover of *The Sporting News,* compared with Harmon Killebrew. The bleacher fans had adopted him as the most popular player, and they adored his every move in the outfield.

"By June 1, I had fifteen home runs and over fifty RBIs," he recalls. "I was having a Mark McGwire-type rookie season."

"In July I went into a real bad slump, but finally came out of it and had a great stroke back. Then one night I swung at a pitch and blew out my knee. My cleats got caught. My foot held steady but my knee twisted. The kneecap and ligaments were damaged. It was the beginning of the end of my career."

He was six feet tall, 195 pounds. Mickey Mantle size. But it was, essentially, all over on that one swing; so fragile can a career really be.

Danny continued to pound out a living in pro ball, but he would never again be a star. He was traded so often, sent to the minors so often, that when he finally made his last major-league plate appearance, with the Texas Rangers in 1980, few in Texas had any idea that this was the one-time Milwaukee hero. It had been so long ago.

Danny wound up with seventeen home runs for 1970. In the rest of his major-league career he added eleven to that number.

"Actually," he says, "one of those eleven was the most memorable moment of my career. I was with Minnesota in 1975 and Frank Quilici sent me up to pinch-hit for Tony Oliva. It was the first time in Oliva's career that he was pinch-hit for. His knees were really bothering him. I stepped up to the plate with the bases loaded and hit a grand slam. It was quite a thrill.

"I'm not a real avid fan today," he says from his home in Los Alamos, New Mexico. "I'm a doer, not a watcher. If I can't participate, I don't want to be involved."

Danny, now forty, moved from Albuquerque in 1984 to shorten his commute to work. "I have a small business at my house and I also work for a company owned by Pan American," he says. "When people around here want to talk baseball with me, I always have more than enough time now. I'm like a kid in that regard; it's never a bother.

"My boy plays Little League baseball, and the other kids will often ask me for advice. That brings back great memories. I still play softball, but I'd rather swing at a fastball than a slow-pitch softball.

"I saved some stuff along the way. I've got the bat I got my first National League hit with. It was 1976 with the Dodgers, and my hit broke up a no-hitter in the eighth inning being thrown by Tom Seaver. I have my bat from the Albuquerque team in 1977. I led the Pacific Coast League with forty-two home runs that year."

Danny went to an Old Timers' Game in Milwaukee in 1986. He saw some old friends he hadn't seen in ten or fifteen years.

"I saw Mike Hegan, Ken Sanders, Marty Pattin, Dave May . . . the game really brought back many memories.

"If I had to do it all over again, I'd change absolutely nothing. I prided myself at the way that I played and worked hard at the game. If I hadn't hurt my knee I would have had a helluva career. I played sixteen years of pro ball and had a great time."

CONCLUSION

*T*he transformation from base-
ball hero to "average man" could not be an easy one. When
the cheering fades, it's usually with a sharp suddenness.
Few players make a "farewell tour" like Carl Yastrzemski
or Stan Musial. Most get handed a terse notice of release,
either after a season or during one last spring training. They
quietly walk back into the clubhouse to gather up their shoes
and gloves, maybe some other personal items, get in their
cars, and drive off to the rest of their lives. As glorious as
it was to be a big-leaguer, the end for most is a difficult
moment.

At home there's the awkward period of embarrassment, explaining to people that your services were no longer desired. Some will say with a smile, "I knew it was time to quit." Others may spend a few years feeling bitter about the circumstances. But while that is going on, the player, still young by working-world standards, must carve out a new career.

A book of this sort twenty years from now will be dealing with players of equal stature but of great wealth. One wonders what is in store for this generation of well-paid athletes. Chris Chambliss, for one, wasted no time looking for work. "I can't just sit home," he said.

They may settle into "average" lives, but unlike the rest of us, their glamorous past always is with them. They may have seen autographing as a chore while active; today it recalls happy times and for a moment makes them feel important again.

Our first jobs out of school were hardly this exciting. The civil servant, the salesman, the construction worker, the accountant, the teacher hardly spend their later years daydreaming about the kind of excitement these fellows experienced. Is that fleeting memory with them at least once a day?

In most cases, no. But it's always waiting to be tapped. Rusty Torres sits in Yankee Stadium with his father, anonymous to the crowd, but hopeful that maybe someone might recognize him. Maybe someone might even give him a chance at a new career.

And maybe, like so many of the success stories in this book, the new career will blend happy memories with bright tomorrows.